Joe Kamiya:
Thinking Inside the Box

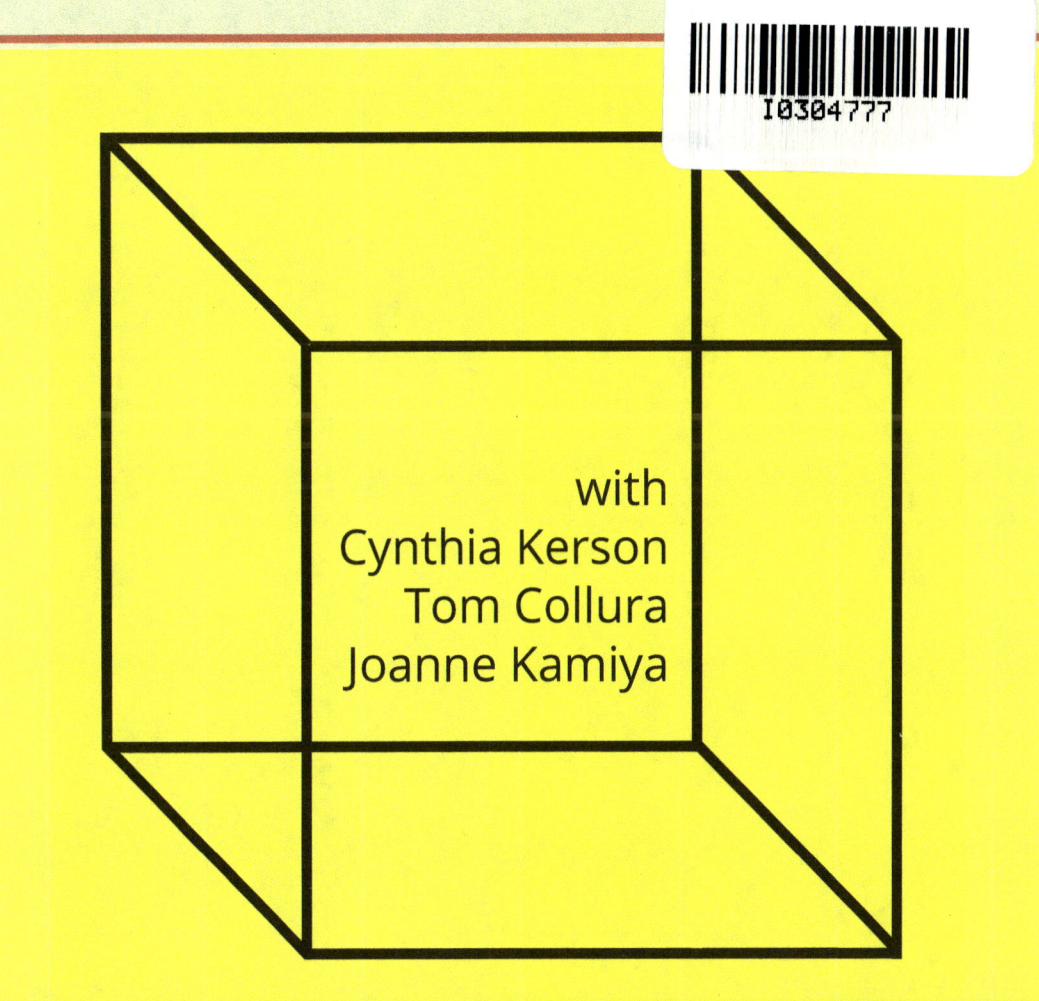

with
Cynthia Kerson
Tom Collura
Joanne Kamiya

Forewords by
James Johnston
& Gary Kamiya

Joe Kamiya:

Thinking Inside the Box

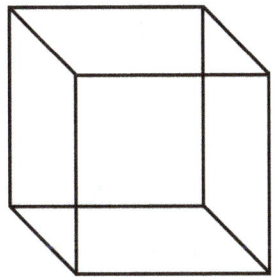

Joe Kamiya:

Thinking Inside the Box

Cynthia Kerson, Tom Collura, Joanne Kamiya

Forewords by
James Johnston & Gary Kamiya

Copyright: 2020 by Cynthia Kerson

All Rights Reserved

Published by:
BMED Press LLC
5402 S. Staples St., Suite 200,
Corpus Christi, TX, USA 78411
(817) 400 – 1639 or www.bmedpress.com

Joe Kamiya: Thinking Inside the Box is a publication of Applied Psychophysiology Education (APEd). Opinions expressed herein are those of the authors and editors and do not necessarily reflect the official view of APEd.

No part of this book may be reproduced, translated, stored in a retrieval system, or transmitted in any way, form, means electronic, mechanical, photocopying, microfilming, or otherwise without express permission from the Publisher.

Printed in the United States of America

ISBN: 978-1-7349618-0-5
Illustrator: Kristina Vukmirovic, Serbia
Book layout and design: Rosalie Blazej, San Francisco, CA, USA

Contact the authors:
Cynthia Kerson: cynthiakerson@gmail.com
Tom Collura: tomc1@brainmaster.com

For my colleagues, friends, and family, because there are some things in life that "show me the data" simply cannot resolve. And especially to my grandsons Clae and Knox, who I hope someday read this and deepen their understandings of life, love and family.

—CYNTHIA KERSON

Joe Kamiya is a truly unique individual, not just for his contributions and his intelligence, and his wit, but also for his humility and his humor. For all the effect he has had on the world, he remains truly in wonder and appreciation, taking no spotlight or glory. He has said that he always wanted to be "a good boy," and he has shown what it means to take this to the limit, to become not just a good man, but a great man.

—TOM COLLURA

Contents

Foreword
James Johnston 1

Foreword
Gary Kamiya 6

Chapter 1
Four Travelers 9

Chapter 2
Joe's Childhood 13

Chapter 3
Joe in Chicago 21

Chapter 4
Joe in San Francisco 27

Chapter 5
Joe and Joanne Meet 32

Chapter 6
Joe Busy at Work 36

Chapter 7
The Future 46

Chapter 8
Some Colleagues 78

Chapter 9
Funding and Research 88

Chapter 10
Philosophical Musings 100

Chapter 11
Thinking Inside the Box 115

Chapter 12
The EEG, QEEG, and
Neurofeedback 125

Joe's Publications 131

Foreword

James Johnston

The first time I watched Joe run an alpha feedback session (in the 1970s) I was "hooked."

While teaching graduate quantum physics (1968-1970), with a focus on macroscopic quantum coherence as a post-doc at Dalhousie University, in Halifax, Nova Scotia, I read a book, "Turning On" by Rasa Gustaitis. The last chapter was about Joe Kamiya and his introduction and riveting explorations of EEG alpha feedback. During summer breaks, I visited him at the University of California, San Francisco (UCSF). (His lab, originally at Langley-Porter Institute, was soon moved to UCSF). After returning to the USA, I taught physics at San Diego State College for three semesters, visiting Joe, when I could.

The first time I watched Joe run an alpha feedback session (in the 1970s) I was "hooked."

The alpha feedback protocol involved a subject sitting in a special isolated room, with lights turned off, and experiencing a series of "trials," each involving (1) a feedback tone presented for 120 seconds, with the volume of the tone representing the strength of the alpha waves over the subject's left occipital lobe, (2) the tone turned off, and a five second display of the average strength of the measured alpha during the 120 second trial, and (3) five seconds of neither sound nor display. These automatically generated trials were repeated for roughly 20 minutes. Then a light was turned on in the subject room, and Joe entered and conversed with the subject about his attempts and experience of the feedback task. His conversation with the subject was simple curiosity. It quickly became clear that these conversations, while providing information, more importantly, helped to enhance the subject's internal awareness. Joe's questioning came from his own curiosity; he was teaching by example (a superior way of enhancing the subject's self-awareness and curiosity). After this conversation with the subject, a longer sequence of these trials, followed by a final conversation with the subject, completed the feedback session.

I had met the ultimate scientist. Joe had clear understanding of the questions he posed, creativity in designing experiments to address those questions, an ego-less pursuit of understanding, and a clear warm way of questioning subjects, that draws them into the exploration. (Thus, they became part of the team of explorers.) I could not resist; I asked Joe to let me join his endeavor and he said, "Yes." (I did not realize, then, the depth and breadth that this "gift" would become for me.)

While working with Joe, I did not speak often about my awareness that my Ph.D. dissertation topic [1967-1968, macroscopic quantum coherence in superfluids is the same as macroscopic quantum coherence in lasers]; and my work with Joe involved alpha coherence in brainwaves, that is related to "coherence" in one's mental state. Sometimes reality is like a poem.

Joe's investigation of EEG alpha feedback began at the University of Chicago in the late 1950s, roughly seven years before he moved to San Francisco. Watching the measurement and analysis of EEG done there, he pondered the question: "Could a subject learn to control the abundance of their EEG alpha that is dominant when the eyes are closed?"

Sometime in the late 1950s to early 1960s, Joe moved to San Francisco and became professor of medical psychology at UCSF's Department of Psychiatry. He was responsible for advising pre-and post-doctoral students from a variety of fields: medicine, physiology, psychology, anthropology, and other specialties, as well as directing his lab at UCSF.

In the early years at UCSF/Langley-Porter, interdisciplinary studies were encouraged by a federally sponsored training and lecture series called the Interdisciplinary Training Program (ITP). Students and faculty attended ITP seminars once a month. Attendees included graduate students and post-doctoral fellows from Japan, England, France and Germany, etc. They were a diverse, bright and interesting group of scientists drawn by interest in Joe's work, and the supportive environment he provided. Joe recognized special qualities in individuals, regardless of age or formal credentials. One example was a very bright young man in his late teens at the time who was active in risky political protests and passionate about social justice. Avram Miller was a welcome contributor to our group and later served as vice-president of Intel Corporation.

When I joined Joe in 1973, his team was Pete Harris, who was a designer of the suite of program-elements for a real-time-system for data acquisition, analysis, and feedback (on an old PDP-15 computer); Dennis Hall, and Joanne Gardner (soon-to-be wife of Joe), in charge of subjects and their reports; and Jack Klinglehoffer, in charge of all electronics and the corresponding structure of data processing. Joe got some grants from Langley-Porter Institute at the UCSF, so that I could work with him. This was the beginning of my deep respect and friendship with Joe and Joanne.

At the time I joined Joe's team, federal support for ITP and the lab was waning. After Pete Harris and Dennis Hall left, I took on the task of completing Pete's beautifully designed home-made real-time system (RTS) for data acquisition and feedback (all written laboriously in the detailed machine language of the PDP-15 computer). This was a new, and significant, challenge for me (e.g., involving many late-night drawings of large flowcharts on butcher paper spread out on the floor of the lab until I began to get a sense of the process.) We are all thankful that Jack stayed for a longer time. He was responsible for the incredibly creative design of the electronic processing of physiological data, and was irreplaceable in the redesign and expansion of data processing that occurred before he left.

Using spare logic cards for the PDP-15 computer, Jack designed a "digital controller" to provide computer control of various aspects of a feedback trial (e.g., turning on or off the digital display of alpha production in a feedback trial and much more!). To the amazement and gratitude of us all, he found a way to accommodate variations in electronic and computer support for all experiments designed by the lab and various guest experimenters, and students.

In order to reorganize the connections between electronic devices, polygraphs, etc., Jack introduced the use of a "rack" and "plug-boards" (used in some kind of sophisticated computer-electronic device combinations, not known to us) to provide laboratory configurations required for "guest" researchers. (We were all in awe of his creativity here!)

All the required inputs and outputs of electronic equipment, polygraphs, computers, etc., are connected to a "rack" that is mounted in a space in a computer bay. This rack is roughly one foot squared, with a roughly 20x20 array of electrical connectors. (We do not remember the exact numbers, here.)

New equipment is added simply by connecting their inputs and outputs to the rack. For each experiment, there is a "plug-board" that has a roughly 11-inch square of non-conducting material in a metallic frame, with an array of holes in the non-conducting panel, matching the array of connectors in the rack. For each experimental setup, desired connections are drawn on a printed (to scale) map of the connections in the rack. The paper map is placed on a plugboard, and plugboard wires are punched through the map into it. This is to connect the output of a device with the input of another in accord with the experimental design. When the plugboard is inserted into the rack, all the desired connections are made to/between the equipment indicated in the paper map.

How did Jack know to create this? To this day, I am awed by this design. One can "create" a laboratory specific to their own experiment, connecting equipment and computer inputs and outputs that are accessible in the rack. Jack created this and I got to play with it! Through the many years Joe's lab was operational students and other researchers were able to create their own experiments and explore their own questions.

When the research expanded beyond eyes-closed alpha feedback, eyes-open EEG was a challenge. The strong bioelectrical nature of the eyeball causes EOG (electrooculogram) artifacts in the EEG due to the eye movements such as saccades (horizontal) and vertical, (mild), and blinks (huge), in the EEG.

Joe had the idea that subtracting recorded EOG from the EEG might reduce the EOG contamination. With electrodes placed above and below one eye, it was clearly possible to reduce the large eye blink artifact significantly, by subtracting a fraction of the vertical EOG from the EEG. This significantly reduced the huge artifact in the EEG due to eye-blinks. This success led to the use of vertical EOG from one eye for blinks (and vertical eye movement), and horizontal EOG from the other eye, in a minimum error-searching algorithm for each, and use of sliding data windows to reduce the "computational load' of the computer algorithms. We were very pleased with the cleanliness of the artifacted EEG. It was Joe's idea; I got to play with and enhance it.

Also, Jack had built an electronic "digital interface' for controlling automated aspects of experiments (e.g., timed control of the feedback tone, the 5-second display of amount of alpha produced, etc. (For this, he used spare logic cards from the PDP-15 computer.) Eventually, as the experimental protocols grew in complexity, Jack's digital interface needed to be updated. He built a new one, suited to the expanded protocols that had evolved (with some feedback from the rest of us). Unfortunately, soon after we developed this work Jack left.

Sometime after this, a library tape for Fortran was discovered. Modification of the PDP-15 operating system, and an interface for libraries, was required to install it. In machine language (involving the individual instructions of the computer processing) the calculation of a Gaussian distribution could take a page or more of machine language code. In Fortran, it involves a single line like:

$$F(x) = exp(-x**2)$$

Special Fortran subroutines, or functions, were created for simple specification of electronic connections and the mathematical processing required for an experiment, for communication between a user and the Real-Time System during the experiment, and for mathematical processing of data. This provided a rich interface between student or guest and the RTS for design of their own projects, with the detailed connections to the RTS hidden from view. The language for control of an experiment, and mathematical processing was English—not machine language. This was especially valuable for graduate students and others doing their own research in this lab. (Much of the technical details were then hidden from them.)

It was an exciting time leading to many threads of research by researchers in Joe's lab. I felt, and still feel, very lucky to have been a part of this. Also, there was a special kind of warm-hearted curiosity that was inspiring—and teasing between us. E.g., in the earlier years in the lab, Joe and I smoked cigarettes—sometimes both at the same time, other times one or the other, or not at all. When smoking, I kept an extra pack in the lab, so I would not run out when (as usual) I worked late at night. When I was smoking, and he wasn't (mostly)—occasionally, when he was working late, and I wasn't, he would find my hiding place, and smoke one of my cigarettes. This led me to find secret hiding places in the lab. He would always find my hidden cigarettes. In this game, he always won. [A couple of "boys" playing with each other. (Precious!)]

On two occasions, there was not enough money to pay me. So, twice, I moved into Joe's basement bedroom (that his eldest son, Tad, had used in the past). This was a very special gift to me; I became a part of Joe and Joanne's family. (Dinner conversation was often very special, regarding both personal and lab topics.) And, I spent time with Joe and Joanne's son Mark (born after I had joined the lab). This has been an incredible gift to me.

— JAMES JOHNSTON

Foreword

Gary Kamiya

[W]hat I take away from Joe's dogged persistence in seeking those big answers is something that is perhaps just as important: asking the big questions.

Joe Kamiya is a great scientist. And as I can attest from personal experience, he is also a great father. Those two things are inextricably connected. Some of the same qualities that made Joe a pioneer in extending the frontiers of our knowledge of consciousness—open-mindedness, patience, curiosity, playfulness, a childlike spirit—also made him a wonderful father. His fellow scientists will write Joe's name on the honor roll of the explorers of inner space. But for my siblings and me, Joe will always be enshrined in an even more important place: as our dad.

Joe met my mother, Dorothy Alford, when they were both students at U.C. Berkeley. They got married in 1950 and had three children: Tad (born 1951), Gary (born 1953) and Janet (born 1957). After Joe and Dorothy got divorced in 1962, Joe married Joanne Gardner in 1970; their son Mark was born in 1973.

Joe has a unique combination of qualities. On the one hand, he's a shy, hard-working, low-key, I-can-take-this-tractor-apart-and-put-it-back-together Japanese farm boy. On the other hand, he's a starry-eyed philosopher and seeker after ineffable truths—a "long-distance dreamer," to borrow the memorable self-description of architect Bernard Maybeck. Throw in a healthy dose of playfulness, and an utterly innocent spirit, that's Joe. He's sui generis.

Those traits manifested themselves in some unusual ways when we were growing up. In a completely benign and fun way, he used to turn his children into guinea pigs in various odd little experiments/games he would dream up. For example, once before we went to bed he told us that if we could fall asleep in half an hour, he would give us $5. Naturally, the thought of that vast sum made it completely impossible for us to fall asleep. As I heard his footsteps approaching, I shut my eyes hard and pretended to be asleep. I heard him enter the room and stand next to the bed. After what seemed an eternity, he let out a soft, mocking laugh. I couldn't restrain myself and chuckled. When I opened my eyes, he explained to me that it was obvious I was pretending to be asleep because the muscles in my face were too tight. "When people fall asleep their faces get completely relaxed," he explained. It was a bit painful having the $5 pulled away at the last minute, and being laughed at on top of it, but it was impossible to be mad about it—and I even learned something about the human physiognomy during sleep.

There were many other examples of Joe's inveterate playful experimenting—some of them no longer socially acceptable or even legal. Joe has always loved animals, and one of our favorite excursions was to the San Francisco Zoo. He would sometimes bring along a small beach ball, which in those free and easy days he would toss into the primate enclosures. We would be riveted, watching the orangutans and chimps playing with the ball until one of them would bring an abrupt and deflating end to the experiment by sitting on it. What Joe communicated to us by engaging in that admittedly non-hygienic practice was his endless curiosity about the world and the creatures in it. It was a kind of neutral observation that was at the same time deeply affectionate. And Joe brought those same qualities to his work as a scientist. Philosophy means love of wisdom, and he had that love. People have always sensed that about him, and it draws them to him.

Joe has always been a supportive, empathetic dad, in a low-key, non-demonstrative, figure-it-out-for-yourself way that I think of as being characteristic of his fellow Nisei (second-generation Japanese-Americans). But as he has gotten older, he has become increasingly interested in the social aspects of being human, and more open to his own emotions. He often speaks about how important his relationship with Joanne, and his earlier one with Dorothy, and being a father to his children has been to his life. Of course, Joe being Joe, this insight is simultaneously emotional and intellectual. He'll say "Having you kids was the most important thing I've done in my life," and then take that into a consideration of just how human social interaction is hardwired into us and has affected our development as a species, and other foundational questions of the sort he has been asking his whole life.

I'm not spoiling the end of the metaphysical movie when I point out that neither Joe or anyone else has come up with answers to those questions. They're philosophical ones, too big and deep for our present state of knowledge. And perhaps they will always be too big to be answered empirically. But what I take away from Joe's dogged persistence in seeking those big answers is something that is perhaps just as important: asking the big questions. As the poet said, A man's reach should exceed his grasp, or what's a heaven for?

You're the greatest, dad. But I'm still going to win that $5 from you.

Gary Kamiya was a co-founder and longtime executive editor of Salon.com and author of the bestselling book "Cool Gray City of Love: 49 Views of San Francisco."

Chapter 1
Four Travelers

Our knowledge of anything is related to other knowledge in other fields. We all need to learn our cognitive map and need to share that with others. That is my shtick nowadays. What the heck are you two doing?

How we remember meeting Joe:

CYNTHIA: The first time I met Joe was at a regional meeting of the Biofeedback Society of California (BSC) where I presented on electrodermal activity. I think it was 2003. I was still quite new to presenting and very nervous. To my fright, Joe was in the audience. I was sure he would discovery me a fraud. Well, he didn't. In fact, he praised my talk and made a couple of reassuring comments and suggestions.

Over these pursuing years, and because Joe and I live in California, we have had many opportunities to meet up. As time went on, Joe lamented that he would like to document his story and I always encouraged him to do so. He said his son, Gary Kamiya, was going to help him. Gary is a very well-respected writer in the Bay Area and I was hopeful to see this life's dream come to fruition. But he lamented and lamented until I finally broke down and said, "Let's do this." Because Tom has been a strong proponent of Joe's and a good friend to both of us, I asked him to participate. The three of us, along with Joe's brilliant and delightful wife, Joanne, met almost weekly for over 2 years; I had only met Joanne once or twice before these conversations at conference functions and dinners. We have hours and hours of recorded conversations. We hope those curated tell Joe's story in a way that helps you to know Joe in the way he would like you to know him and also for you to learn and grow from his experience and message. This will always be one of the luckiest projects of my career.

TOM: Terri and I met Joe at the AAPB Annual Meeting in Las Vegas in March of 2002 when he came by our exhibit to see our latest compact EEG, try on a headset, and share coffee and a sandwich. We immediately struck up a series of conversations that quickly went beyond the nuts and bolts of the equipment, and into the nature of consciousness and related topics. We continued over the years to discuss what it is to be human, the nature of awareness, and the possibilities of enhancing awareness of the brain and mind. Joe has the most generous, patient, and welcoming personality we have ever encountered. He is one of the few people with whom one can feel safe to discuss one's wildest thoughts ranging from brain machines to the future of humanity, and points in between. We were privileged to help organize some panels and talks at FutureHealth, ISNR, and AAPB meetings, developing Joe's ideas on "first-person science," and the possibilities of mapping out consciousness the way we map out the physical world, using science and systematic methods to explore inner space.

Joe presented the keynote dinner talk at the ISNR-RF FriendRaiser in 2013. By not limiting EEG feedback to therapeutic or remedial applications, we envisioned ways to expand consciousness and change the path of human development, as the evolved creature studied its own evolution. In Joe's view, the awareness of the brain and mind, and the understanding of self-regulation, should be a key part of education for all children. After several of such presentations, the opportunity presented itself to create the "ISNR Joe Kamiya Award for First-Person Science," allowing us to come "out of the closet" and recognize contributors in this area of study. Many others have been instrumental in supporting Joe and these ongoing efforts to get the word out. When the time seemed ripe to take another step, it was an honor to be able to work with Joe, Joanne, and Cynthia on this new volume, which should continue to get the word out, and to inspire others to pursue this valuable and critical branch of a continually new science.

Joe Kamiya: Good morning. I ponder what do I want to do with the rest of my life. A very interesting question, no real answer to it, keeps you wondering. So, anyhow, it's wonderful to hear from you.

Tom Collura: Well, you know, Joe, we've talked for years, probably about 10 years, about the first-person science, and gaining some recognition; you've given some beautiful panel talks and speeches. We have some of those recorded, and we just find them so valuable. Cindy and I are both so interested in this topic, that what we want to do is, if you are willing and able to have a conversation with us on a regular sort of basis, use that to comprise a book of them.

JK: Tom, what you have to do so I can follow your speech, is to slow down a bit because I missed some of the words that you're saying at the rate you're speaking. Keep your words separate and reasonably clear.

TF: OK. We're interested in having a dialogue with you and learning some things that we can write about and help you publish some of your deeper most important thoughts.

JK: Are you speaking of a joint effort between you and me or do you think you want to write down things for yourself?

TF: Oh no! This is your work and we want to help as interviewers and to help write things down. But this is your book. We would like to help you with your book.

JK: OK. So yes.

Joanne Kamiya: Joe are you picking up on this?

JK: Well I think I am.

JoK: Joe, they want to do a series of interviews and just to have some discussions about once a week to get your thoughts and ideas and part of a history and development of some of those ideas down so that it can be put out to the public. OK, Joe?

JK: OK. Thank you. Well, would you like me to start right now?

Cynthia Kerson: Yes!

JK: Our knowledge of anything is related to other knowledge in other fields. We all need to learn our cognitive map and need to share that with others; that is my shtick nowadays. What the heck are you two doing?

TC: I am president with AAPB. Cindy has a brilliant chapter in a book Jon Frederick, and I are editors of. I see clients for NFB and counselling.

JK: Cindy, what are you doing?

CK: I'm not in clinical practice anymore; we moved to the Napa Valley 5 months ago. I have many projects. I'm professor at Saybrook University. I work to help others get certification in biofeedback, neurofeedback and QEEG through my company APEd.

JK: You are in my neck of woods?

Chapter 2
Joe's Childhood

"Interesting thing—in my life as a junior and senior in high school, I recognized I was in a depression. I was unhappy, remember going to my agriculture teacher and told him, "I don't know what the problem is. What is my purpose, what am I?"

JK: I've begun to ponder to myself, what do I want to do with the rest of my life? That's a very interesting question.

CK: I bet the last time you asked yourself that, it was right before you went to college.

JK: That's right. It's kind of a nice question to ask because there is no real answer to it, and it keeps you alive and wondering.

OK. I think that one of the very interesting things in my life is that as an adolescent, oh, maybe 12- or 13-years-of-age. I may have been a junior or senior in high school. I began to wonder what life is, and what it means, and I was very concerned because I did not know the answer. I thought it was something that could be analyzed and thought and resolved but I didn't recognize that I was in the kind of a depression I was in. And I don't know exactly how that originated. Perhaps it was because my father died when I was six years of age, and though I had siblings, older siblings, and my mother of course, we all got along pretty well, of course there were some fisticuffs as kids and so on, I was quite unhappy.

And I remember going to my high school agriculture teacher whom I loved. This was in the country and agriculture was one of the topics that a special teacher was hired to do, the schools had federal grants programs. I went and told him I don't know what the problem is for me, but I keep asking myself what life is about, what is its purpose, what am I trying to do? And it bothers me because no one else seems to be bothered about such things. And so that's how I spoke, and he listened, and then he reached up on the shelf, and he had a volume written by a Harvard philosopher named Ernest Hocking, called "Philosophy for the Farmer." And that book was not helpful at all, it didn't seem to speak to anything of the sort that I was concerned with. He was much more worldly or something or another. He was a little bit too abstract and adult for me, to be able to fully comprehend. But I appreciated the effort; I loved the man. He was a guy who was quite concerned, and he used to praise my work as a student in an agricultural project.

I raised chickens. I had 600 laying hens by the time I went through about two or three years of buying day-old baby chicks and raising them and then hatching them to become good egg productive laying hens. I had bulletins from the Department of Agriculture—both from the State of California and from the Federal government, and my ag teacher found that I had a little brown volume that I had made keeping the various bulletins in. I had taken it to school one day, and he found it on my desk. He grabbed it and immediately went to the head of the class and held them up in the air and he told the rest of the class what a wonderful thing this was that I had taken so much interest in this field. And that kind of thing, of course, was tremendous for me, I was very proud of course. That was interesting that here, at least, was one guy who wasn't going to discourage me, that was willing to help. But I had no answers.

When I spoke to you just a few minutes ago earlier, I was beginning to wonder what life was about, is there a certain way of readdressing some of these questions. Now that I am 91 years old, I can get back to some of these questions. I think that there is no depression going with me this time, it seems that it is something that, and I see that the depression I had, each person can and must confront in themselves in different ways and it is something that adds to the richness of this thing that we call life. So, anyhow, that's sort of the starting point that got me going. I have not seriously looked at it since, except maybe one or two years into college. Maybe when I was still in college, I started a journal of my own thoughts about things. I stopped about when I went into college. I'm not even sure I have it around. But it would be a gold mine for me if I did find it because it shows the struggles of a teenager coming face to face.

I suspect that part of my problems originated because of my ethnicity. In many ways I had many reactions to the fact that I was an Asian in a Caucasian world when I was a kid. It's not as though I was totally rejected by any of my peers because of my ancestry, but there was always some awareness that there was a white kid and there was a Japanese kid and that somehow or other, the way I reacted to this is perhaps best likened to what psychologist Kurt Lewin said and wrote about being Jewish. He wrote about self-hatred among Jews referring to the fact that their minority status and their explicit and often implicit rejection of themselves by the established majority led them to begin hating their own identity because it meant that they were kept out of some of the positive, the rewards of life, the pleasures, et cetera. And that article was very informative to me, because I recognized that, yes, I had developed a certain self-hatred of the fact that I was Japanese, because of the fact that I was in a minority, which was not explicitly so among my peers, but kind-of in the more culturally broader sense, that I was a sort-of a minority person and the realization that I was a minority in the personal sense. There was certainly reason for me to be aware of the rejection because it became U.S. policy in WW2 when they decided to confine all of us to relocation centers (so called) away from the state of California. It was a mass incarceration of 100,000 people or so. There were camps in the Western United States, you probably know something about that. But, by-God that certainly was a clear, explicit, face-to-face confrontation that I had with my own ancestry and its place in this country.

So anyway, as a kid I grew up doing, as a thing, developing racist slurs about myself and my buddies—who would do the same, I called myself a Jap. A Swede called himself a lousy Swede. We developed a kind-of a joking relationship about our different ancestry. I wish to Hell I had documented exactly what I had called myself and my friend as we walked on our way to school.

Another guy, we called Dutch because his parents, well his ancestors, came from Holland perhaps three or four generations ago. The Swedish kid was also two or three generations born. I was the first American-born generation among the Japanese. I'm sure that had something to do with my whole personality and disposition and outlook on life and so on. I'm quite impressed that the social vectors that prevail in the life, where there is some kind of inequality status, profoundly can affect an individual and the way he grows up. And the fact that I consider myself, proudly, an American, and I'm thoroughly enjoying my life in this country and I would say, it's a good thing about our country, that it does this. I think we are probably more advanced than any other country in the world as far as acceptability by different people of each other's ancestry. I think that aspect of things is certainly worth mentioning when I talk about my own life.

CK: Joe, how would you tie in the notion of cellular memory tie into your experience? The notion that our DNA changes with every memory we consume, that our experience further ties us to our ancestry and changes us as we develop.

JK: I must say to you—on that one: this notion, I haven't given any concern about that. Or even thought about how DNA plays a role in this kind of thing that I find in myself or thought of how that works.

JoK: Joe, you talk about evolution so much. This is, again, I think, directed towards the evolution of a single person.

JK: I certainly do think that our understanding of our evolution from prehuman to human and our development as social creatures is a very profound truth that deeply roots our nature such that we would be quite nonfunctional, and we suddenly would find ourselves to be completely isolated from our peers. Imprisonment must be a supreme form of torture, except for the fact that you see a guy come in 3 times a day to feed you, and maybe you can talk to a neighbor or another jail mate. But that is an incredibly cruel thing to do to a human being. Which is not recognized because the concern is more about the danger of the individual to the world and also a fair amount of rejection of antisocial activity and their punishments – that are considered to be quite appropriate. In fact, when you think about it, it's a form of social control that has evolved through time that I think has severe shortcomings for the development of a human being. I think we are, some of us, some people are recognizing this and the way we handle antisocial behavior is a very important kind of component of social policy and politics.

Well, anyway, I have myself been mildly speculative of myself in terms of the evolution of human beings. I find it very breathtaking to realize that: Here I am, speaking to another human being about the forces of our very consciousness. We are evolved from simple forms of single cells which reacted completely and automatically, according to things. Socialization was a very early development, even in simple forms. It meant that reproduction involved other people. We did not evolve by sort-of self-generating our own genes.

We are the byproduct of a single mating with another human being and our current situation is one that is very remarkable. When you think about it, we developed, let's say, from ant colonies to New York City residents. It's simply mind-blowing when you think about the course of evolution which has taken us to where we are.

CK: Please speak about your personal first-person experience in your own exploration.

JK: It was very adolescent, and I began to get very concerned about what life was all about. And I began to think of it as a logical problem somehow. And it depressed me in that I wasn't getting any clear answers to myself. And I felt especially unhappy because there were these questions like: What is the meaning of life? Why am I here? And so on.

I apparently felt recognized, but that was part of the depression I had felt, yet I hadn't contemplated anything like suicide, but this made me feel totally, completely lost especially because none of my peers seemed to give a damn about this. I enjoyed myself just as much as the others on the school bus on the way to school—pulling the girls' hair in the seat in front of me. But somehow or other, that seemed rather hollow to me and I felt, all along, in the struggle in discovering the meaning of life. Yes, I could pull the girl's hair in this seat of the bus in front of us and I could get a response out of her and I had great fun talking about ballgames with my fellow guys. And I was a reasonably competent basketball player on the "C" team, which is the smallest size people at the school. Anyway, my ponderings were related to such things as what is really the meaning of being alive? What are we here for? Why do we go through all this trouble of going to school and all that?

They are still interesting to me, philosophical questions. But now they're more oriented around scientific issues such as what are the brain and body processes that are related to feelings, thoughts, emotions, etc.? And the fact that we are a highly developed social species that can communicate with words means that this complexity is almost certainly to have evolved as a social product of interactions.

And so, this partial realization is what leads me to say that I can only go so far insofar as pondering what are the relationships between consciousness and body and brain. And it would be enormously helpful for me to be able to join with others in raising these questions and talking about them normally and regularly and trying to come to some kind of a building up of a body of, shall we say, knowledge or at least a set of common assumptions about what we're after.

Anyhow, while I tried to get into that. It didn't help very much because the sort-of existential quandary I was in, it did not address very adequately. Especially to someone like me—an academic type.

I struggled with that all through high school and even in college. I often struggled with things not being clear—about what everything was about. I didn't have much luck talking to others. I did once speak to the general secretary of the Heritage Foundation, which was the liberal arm of the YMCA that was active in social issues. He was nice personally; a friendly person and he could only assure me that things would be fine. He didn't help much either. Fortunately, I met other people that I could relate to—especially people of the opposite sex.

This made a significant difference for me and I suddenly realized that I was not facing this in this world, but part of a larger world and if I were to specifically take part in that larger world. . . In short, I realized I was very much a social person and here I'm referring to a species characteristic – the social person. Everybody is and everyone is very dependent on the context of social interaction. And I found that I enjoyed the company and contact of personal relationships of others. So, looking back on it all—and this emerged when my father died, and I was six-years-old. It was some kind of parental or some kind of contact or some kind of supervision or some other thing that might have helped me avoid that.

That kind of pondering, I came to remember, as thinking that a life that is not pondering deeper meaning is not a life that's being fully lived. I was a very introspective person (without fully recognizing that term as being applicable to me—but me being just an isolated person). I was very concerned with this question. And I do believe that one of the things that led me to the study of EEG, through the study of dreams, at the University of Chicago, was my first year as an academic instructor—across the street from me was the lab run by William Dement on all the facets of dreams, such as the types and number of dreams and how people dreamed, etc., and by watching the EEG and the movement of the eyes.

When you think about it, the business of introspection, which is what differentiates humans from all other creatures in a way. We think—but that we don't know about yet because we don't know if animals introspect. But they may engage in thinking about themselves in a very primitive manner. For us it is crucial for our happiness. Especially when we run into periods of challenge of various kinds, like illness or loss of friends, or whatever. And for me I know that introspection was the absolute requirement when I was a kid in college or before—in high school. I began to worry or think about what life was all about. What was the purpose of it? What was I doing? And so on. It was a kind of a depression that was unrecognized by me and I guess might've been due to the fact that my father died when I was six-years-old and I would have wonderings about what life was all about, I suppose.

Then too, of course, the culture conflict—the fact that the Japanese were not the most popular people in the US. And the fact that state legislation prevented these immigrants from being naturalized. It was about the time shortly before I was born and there were various kinds of acts of vandalism against some of the Japanese in the community. So, I suspect that kind of thing had something to do with it—the fact that I was a member of a minority. But the important thing is that. . .well, the point I'm trying to make here is that it's a brain process. That's the process of the brain that reflects upon one's place in the world upon one's relationship especially upon one's relationship with others.

And perhaps, though I no longer find myself feeling depressed, that I don't know the answers to these questions, they are still interesting to me. But now they are more oriented around scientific issues such as what are the brain and body processes that are related to feelings, thoughts, emotions, etc. And the fact that we are a highly developed social species that can communicate with words means that this complexity is almost certain to have evolved as a social product of interactions. And so, this partial realization is what leads me to say that I can only go so far in sort of pondering what the relationship between consciousness and body and brain are and that it would be enormously helpful for me to be able to join with others in raising these questions and talking about them normally and regularly and trying to come to some kind of a building-up of a body of, shall we say, knowledge, or at least, several of the common assumptions about what we're after.

Anyway, I wanted to say that going into the whole business of the fact that I am of Japanese descent and grew up in a culture that was not quite yet ready to accept them and where in many cases it was outright discrimination and legal protections against the Japanese immigrants for example in California. It was not until the 1950s that it became possible for Japanese immigrants to become naturalized. And so, you know, I went through that as an adolescent, one with attachments primarily in the dominant white culture because the school was, let's say, three quarters white and only one quarter Japanese. Therefore, I had more acquaintances among the whites than I did among the Japanese. And I went through much of what Kurt Lewin has written about and I may have mentioned this once before.

He talked about, or wrote about, self-hatred among Jews and he showed, or he gave as an example, how one Jewish woman became tremendously uptight when she heard someone else who was being very, very talkative and loud and she was tremendously relieved when she discovered that the woman was not Jewish at all. But you can see how that kind of self-hatred among Jews is a universal sort-of a thing among many of the immigrant children, and even among some of the immigrants themselves.

As they moved into this country and culture and I certainly went through that and began to form my own preferences for the White culture. And if one looked into it, I would suspect that that helped contribute to the fact that Joanne happens to be White. It was probably not an accident.

JoK: Ha, ha. My parents had something to do with it.

But anyway, there is no doubt that I felt sometimes terribly unhappy when some of my fellow Japanese second-generation American kids would begin to speak Japanese at school and I hated that because it marked us off as a different population. And it's interesting to talk right now because of the current controversy with regard to the so-called "dreamer generation"—kids who were brought by parents into this country but are foreign. And now with Trump pumping up about deporting some of those kids, there's a great amount of anxiety and anger about the Trump point of view, which is held, unfortunately, by large numbers of the American population. So anyway, that's one thing.

It was my feeling that the technology of biofeedback—neurofeedback in particular—but all forms of biofeedback, really would be extremely useful to introduce as part of a child's education because the person can do the kind of self-explorations that the technology would permit by simply asking questions and the child can dig in to start using as a diary of ideas that he might ask about things. I guess what I'm thinking about is when I was a teenager, if I was sort of lost and wondered what life was all about and depressed because I couldn't find any immediate answers and I'm not sure I could have articulated what it was in writing what the hell was bugging me, but I think I actually did some—because I had some notes that I discovered later.

When my father had died, I had actually started articulating what the hell it was I was asking about. In any case all of that had, kind of, slipped my mind since our last conversation. And so, I felt shame-facedly helpless. But anyway, it's the sort of thing that has a sort of elusive quality because, even as I speak, I struggle with this interesting cognitive problem right at the moment.

So, I was depressed and wondered what life was all about, and depressed because I could not find any immediate answers. And I'm not sure I could have articulated in writing what the hell it was that was bugging me. But I think I actually did somewhat, because I had some notes that I discovered later and I do remember going to that high school Ag teacher who had sort of befriended me and became kind of a substitute father, I guess, because my father had died when I was six and I thought I had started articulating what it was that I was asking about and in any case, all of that had slipped my mind since our last conversation.

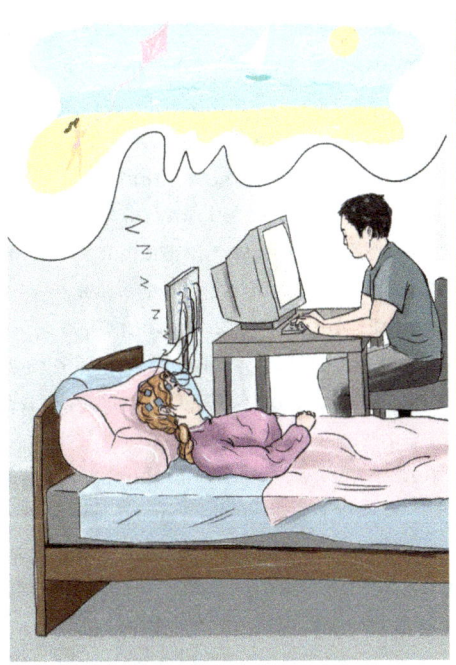

Chapter 3
Joe in Chicago

While at the University of Chicago I was still sometimes finding myself pondering some of the thoughts that I had when I was a kid. Thoughts of existence and what the hell I was doing here at the University of Chicago. Is what I am doing to my students imparting anything valuable to them etc. etc.?

JK: Sleep study, kind of, first attracted me to the EEG, when I was at the University of Chicago in my second year. I discovered that the guy across the street, William Dement, was studying dreams using an EEG. And I was thinking that's kind of interesting. The fact that it attracted me was not unique of course because the whole world was really sitting up and paying attention. A large fraction of the world paid attention to the fact that our dreams could now be tagged, or the dream process, could now be tagged.

And I'm sure that that had a decisive factor for me because I immediately went over and introduced myself to Bill Dement and he was happy. His professor, who was an expert on sleep, was rather aged at the time, and was Bill's academic sponsor. Bill had not yet gotten his PhD. He was in the department of physiology. I was in psychology and was so happy when he agreed to teach me the technology of EEG recording and getting dream reports and so on. And that of course got me curious when I started watching these alpha waves coming and going, always wondering if there was any subjective concomitant convergence. And so, I'm training people to discern the presence or absence of occurrence of an alpha rhythm led to the discovery that, my God, people can learn to discern when they're having an alpha rhythm and as it goes if you're given discrimination training to do so. You know consisting of the standard wave of alpha, when the experimenter sees these signals, ask the subject to guess what and the subject gives the response and the experimenter says he's right or wrong on that.

And the important part that was discovered by me and I'm sure everybody, who was, by then, aware, having learned to discern the difference, I could also learn now to enter into the state. That is to say, to control those that produced alpha or that diminished alpha, or that led to the disappearance of alpha. And so, everybody got all excited about the control factor of course because that's the most important thing in life is to control things. It goes with our culture.

But for me, it's equally important that we can discover our states of mind, at least partially. Because they, believe it or not, correlated, sometimes, with a physiological process that we can tag.

And so, the future is still bright of course in the whole area of how to improve upon the various subjective states or resources with different kinds of technologically definable events in EEG, especially as well as the body processes.

I was thinking about the origins of EEG alpha research in case I didn't say so, it started in the sleep lab in 1954 or so starting with Daniel Kleitman. My purpose at the time, in 1954 or so, was about studying dreams. That was my interest, but what caught my attention early on in the game was the wakeful EEG with its frequent alternations in the EEG. Alpha, as in wakeful alpha that is characterized "awake." Sometimes it would occur as often as 10 or 20 times in a minute and then irregularly as maybe two or three per minute. Those were all more or less individual different markers characterizing a person who was awake and not really ready to go to sleep.

And I got started because of it. While at the University of Chicago I was still sometimes finding myself pondering some of the thoughts that I had when I was a kid of existence and what the hell I was doing here at the University of Chicago. Is what I am doing to my students imparting anything valuable to them etc. etc.?

But also, I happened to notice across the street was the sleep laboratory where Bill Dement and Nathaniel Kleitman were making astounding discoveries about the EEG markers of dreaming sleep and dreaming. And so, this was extraordinarily interesting to me so I was very fortunate because I went over there, and I asked if I could learn some techniques and work in their laboratory. And they said, "Sure" and they taught me how to use the EEG and detect the moments when the person was dreaming. And so, I thought, "This is great."

And it just so happens that in the department of psychology, which is really strongly behavioristic, using operant methodology as the tool into knowledge about human beings -where Howard Hunt held forth. He was a nice guy but very strongly Skinnerian. And one of the things I learned about, and used, in my work with that came about in the following way:

Operant conditioning, you know discrimination training, and you know using reinforcers and so on. I noticed that as I was preparing my dream subjects, my sleeping subjects, while they were still awake would come this alpha rhythm within them—coming and going, coming and going and I got to wondering, "Hey, this is something that's happening inside—in the brain." And so, one day I took one of my sleep and dream subjects, by which time I had managed to get a small NIH grant to study sleep and dreams to help further my interest in sleep.

But while this person is awake, this alpha comes and goes and comes and goes. I asked, "Hey, can I use discrimination training to see if a person can become aware of the presence or absence of alpha? So, I said "OK. Here is what we do." I took the subject and said, "From time to time I will ring the single ding of a bell. Sometimes when you're in state A and sometimes when you are in State B." For me, state A was when alpha was present, and B was alpha absent. And so, I was asking this person to spot the difference between those two by using the words A or B. And, son of a gun, he learned the very first time.

I was always saying "right, right, correct" until I said wrong and he knew then, by God, he really was discerning something. Because by deliberately giving me the wrong response, his teacher—me, said, "Wrong." That was an enlightening experience for both of us, I tell you. It was wonderful.

I still enjoy talking about that because it was a moment of great excitement for me and for him too. Anyway, this discrimination training should go a long ways in furthering the stuff that we're talking about right now. Suppose I get myself into reflections of the nature of who I was, what was happening, who am I. I will maybe sometimes feel as though I am developing some new sense that hasn't been happening before.

But really this began to shape up my interest that awake alpha EEG could be detected in 80% of people without electronic aid, and just the shape of the alpha wave would come and go several times a minute. Sometimes only two or three times but with long trains of alpha and other times in runs.

One of the things I thought I would do, because it seemed a natural question to ask, since I was in a strictly behavioristic school in the department of psychology, was if operant discrimination training might be useful. I tried to train the presence or absence of alpha for subjects in their normal waking pattern. I picked people whose alpha was approximately 50% of the time on and 50% of the time off, roughly. I told a subject, I would from time to time, ring a single ring of a bell sometimes when they were having "state A" and sometimes when they were having "state B."

For me, A was alpha, and B was non-alpha. And I told them to make a guess as to which of the two they were in at the moment and then I would immediately tell them whether they were right or wrong. I proceeded that way with several trials, at least 10 or 20 trials. For about 10 minutes or so. It varied widely with different subjects because of the extent people had alpha. Recall, I found people who had roughly 50% alpha and non-alpha so as to cut down the individual differences. OK. So, I started, I rang the bell sometimes and sometimes not and had them guess and I said right or wrong.

So, I started with my first subject, a student, a junior, and he had beautiful alpha rhythms where they would be clearly present and then clearly absent. We paid $10.00 for him to sleep in the lab. He was the best darn discrimination training subject I ever had. Within one or two sessions he got it correct. I would ring a bell sometimes when the alpha was present and sometimes when it was absent. Usually that means present for one or two seconds.

And son of a gun, my very 1st subject, who I may have said, even to you, that he may have been sent by God because, wow! He was the best subject I ever ran. He learned very quickly. I've forgotten now—in maybe one or two sessions. Maybe even in the first session. But the fact is he got a string of 400 correct trials in a row. At which, I extended the session because this guy was so remarkable to be so accurate. And for a while, this guy thought I was pulling his leg. I was saying correct to everything he said so he deliberately gave a wrong response and when I said, "Wrong," that really shook him up. That really convinced him he was right. And that was great fun and a really remarkable moment because of another factor: if he could get this right all the time, I thought maybe I can teach him to acquire control of his alpha. He knew of its presence or absence, so he might be able to turn it on or off.

So, I began to ask myself could people be trained to be aware of the comings and goings of alpha. And I had learned all about operant discriminant training and so on. So, I thought, "Well, might people be trained to discern the presence of an internal event like a brainwave?" Much like you could train an adult or child to discriminate sights, colors or sounds, etc. so I said, "Hey, very easy to do."

So, I said, "OK, this time, I'm going to do something different. When I ring the bell once, I would like you to try to get into the state you've been calling A and other times I'll ring the bell twice, whereupon I would like you to try to get into the state you've been calling B." Well, lo and behold, this guy, having learned to discriminate alpha from non-alpha, he was immediately able to turn it on and off at will. And, surprisingly, for a long period of time. Much longer than any string of alpha he'd had before or period of State B he'd had before. He had clearly learned an internal state. So, we all asked, "How did you do it?" We immediately realized the wonderful circumstance of operant conditioning of EEG, or, for that matter, many other body functions. Other guys would say, "Gee, I don't know" or sometimes, "Well, sometimes, maybe it's like I'm feeling relaxed" or some would even go to say, "It's a time when I think of my uncle and after that would be alpha."

And later, we query and find out that his uncle was one of the most valued people he knew; he loved him. And this was a state that he didn't realize was a rather calm, nice state. It also happens, I come to find out, that when people think about being in the presence of something nice and friendly, that they tend to produce more alpha. Not necessarily on a systematic basis, though I could well be wrong, it certainly seemed that way. And here's the subjective reports of people, every one of whom I trained. Of course, I'd ask, "What is the state like?" By this time, I had well learned to accept any sort of a sincere effort to try to get it. People would sometimes be stuck for words and have difficulty saying it and would not know quite why and so on. But, in general, I kind of assumed, by the various replies, that alpha was a kind of a calm state and not filled with anxiety about doing the experiment or worrying about something in their life situation. But rather, they were rather calm.

Since I had the experiment done with their eyes closed, it would not equate with their actual visual inspection of the world. And it was very clear to me that when the people decided to suppress alpha all they had to do was to imagine the after-images in their eyeballs for a good close look at the images that streamed around in their eyes, although the eyes had been closed. That inspectional attitude seemed to be very effective to control alpha. It is now known, and has always been known, ever since alpha was first experimented with, that with eyes open, and when reading, is associated with the diminution of alpha. So, that's the back story about alpha and its controls.

Others have reported to me that they've found it useful in doing therapy to calm people down and to get them to be a little more properly settled in the therapeutic situation. One or two people have actually found it useful to actually do it whether or not it was ever done by psychotherapists. Since I don't do psychotherapy, I don't run into people who do it very often, so I don't know what the situation is. It would be an interesting thing to pursue. Certainly, it is known, that training people to relax their EMG on their forehead would be very useful in calming people down or helping them overcome, let's say, insomnia or other sorts of difficulties associated with muscular tension. Certainly, we now know about the control of heart rate, and many other body functions. So that's the end of one long sentence.

CK: Can you speak about how you recruited people. Like, you said, "The first person you worked with, that it was serendipitous. . ."

JK: Generally, my first subjects were the students at University of Chicago. It was convenient for them to come to my lab because they didn't have to walk more than a block or so to get there. And, I also found them very interested in participating, they were quite intrigued by the thought that their own EEG could somehow be discerned by them and that it could be controlled by them was sufficient to motivate them into coming. And so that's how I started.

I've since discovered, having run others as well, among the most important features of the psychological environment for the person, and for me could be that I was assuring of them that this is a task that could be done and that it sometimes may take a little bit more time and that they should not feel discouraged at the first few efforts if they fail to make the correct guess or to produce more alpha. It had to do with being personable, not official to them. I sensed that approach was quite useful.

Subjects types: I was mostly limited to young adults in my studies. I don't know what the story is these days—if there are other age ranges. I just simply have not followed the literature in the field.

CK: How did the university look at your work? Was it difficult for you to get approval, for example with the IRB, (if there were IRBs then)? I wonder how it fit into the culture of where you were teaching.

JK: No problem, my chairman encouraged me.

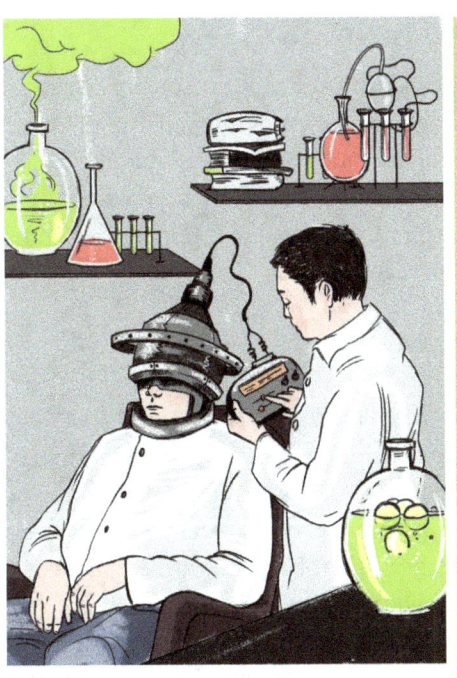

Chapter 4

Joe in San Francisco

When one trains a person to discern a subjective quality—differentiating one brain wave from another, he may actually do little experiments to see what happens when he does this. That is to say, doing private experiments of control in the pursuit of learning discernment.

CK: Let's move on to why you moved to San Francisco.

JK: When we moved to San Francisco, it was around 1960, and I had originally been at UC Berkeley. I worked at University of Chicago for six years, then at UCSF. I much preferred the weather in San Francisco—Chicago is much for the "snowbirds."

And now I'm retired for 10 years. We decided it would be better to move out here due to weather. I am now fully retired. I seem to be happy. I would like to write the story of my life. What would I like to write? I feel like I should.

CK: If you could tell us about San Francisco. At UCSF what did you teach? You met Joanne... Tell us about this time.

JK: When I came to San Francisco, I finished up the grants related to sleep and dreaming. That took a year or two to do. The area of sleep and dreams and the physiology thereof I pretty much left to my idol when I came upon the notion of discerning and controlling EEG and other psychophysiologic measures using biofeedback. That whole process started with discernment of the alpha rhythm and controlling EEG through feedback; to train the discernment and to discriminate the presence or absence of alpha. And getting the subjects to try to articulate verbally what the experience was like. What I found, most interestingly, was that those that learned to discern were now also able, apparently by virtue of the training, to control, to produce the rhythms upon my command. And that aspect of control was much more interesting to the rest of the world than some academic discrimination of brainwaves. Because now people could see how that could be related to the various maladies that could be tagged by the EEG and drowsiness or insomnia.

But all the rest. And of course, it also added to the impetus in the field by others in this area of psychophysiology that was beginning to be called biofeedback. And so, that whole area is now the entire field of applications in therapy. And, we must not forget the tremendous opportunity we have to consider this area as a basic science.

To unearth the relationships between aims, experiences, thoughts, emotions, memories, etc. with what's going on in the body and brain. And that would be the long-range contribution. And which will be, I hope, and I believe will, stimulate hundreds, if not thousands, of scientists all over the world. And we will begin to have a new picture of what we are as human beings and as social creatures, evolved in developing our own brains in interactions with each other and in conversation and in social control and that whole area will begin to be recognized as a basic science of the human being. Period.

TC: I think we share that vision.

JoK: That's where you were headed with first-person science, Joe.

TC: And, still are.

JoK: At UCSF, Sonia Ancoli earned her PhD with Joe and did a review of EEG alpha and so did Ron Laye. He worked with us for a while and then was teaching in British Columbia (I think). There were two compilations of that sort that I might be able to find. They did bibliographies of the work.

The work that Joe did was basically stuff about the different frequencies, and what was associated with those frequencies. Including what I just mentioned about slow-wave potentials. He basically followed his own interests in developing rather small pilot studies to show what people did to discriminate states, how they associated with them, what they had to say about them, and how that all went.

We got a lot of subjects through the lab because of, to our knowledge, what was going on in the EEG Joe was measuring at the time. The slow wave stuff was written up with a guy named Dexter Girton. Maybe we can find some of that. It was interesting. Also, some was with Paul Gorman, who did work with stomach acid feedback. As well, Karen Naifeh did a post doctorate on respiration, EEG, and meditation. Paul did his dissertation under Joe. And, there's lots of stuff like that. But I think we should make a concerted effort to pull that together.

JK: We'll work towards a list of the titles of the papers.

TC: Can you continue with discussing how your work grew and developed in San Francisco?

JK: I need to reflect. I can start the process, but I may have to fill in with things that come to me later. Here's how in unfolded: I landed in San Francisco full of great hopes. And it was my home state and I was to work at the great University of California. I was happy to be able to transfer grants from Chicago to here. During the first weeks I was setting up my lab, I was continuing the alpha studies using an EEG lab that had been not used. Langley Porter had been built only 20 or 30 years earlier and for some reason the shielded room that was set up was apparently used by the research staff (if there was a research staff). There was a clinic downstairs. They also had an EEG room. That was handled by a different guy—I forget his name.

We were on the 3rd floor in the lab with the shielded EEG room, which was perfect for me. So, I continued my research there on discrimination and also observing and verifying the fact that people who learned to discern were able to achieve control. It's an interesting thing. When one trains a person to discern a subjective quality—differentiating one brain wave from another, he may actually do little experiments to see what happens when he does this. That is to say, doing private experiments of control in the pursuit of learning discernment.

I think some people tend to do that as they correctly learn the presence of alpha. And I rang the bell and the choice was alpha or no alpha expressed as A or B, they may begin to say A for alpha sand B for non-alpha. And, as they're doing that, they began to say to themselves, "Hey, what was I doing when A was correct?" So, then they would try whatever they thought they were doing when the A as correct. So, you see, learning discernment seemed intrinsically to involve learning control, also. And that, I think, is an important part to remember because the two are psychologically twin brothers. Or one is, sort of, the role of the other.

Everybody thinks all about control, but when you think of control, as a matter of fact, it's perfectly clear that people who learned what to do, as opposed to doing something else to produce alpha, or beta, or whatever it is that they're asked to do. So, control learning also involved discernment learning. And it's procedurally that the two are differentiable, but what is going on in the person's head, they're twin psychological systems.

CK: I think of them as parallel entities. Where the subjective and objective are integrated. Which came first? The chicken or the egg? Does neither come first?

TC: I've noted that you can have discernment without control. In fact, the whole field of astronomy is built on discernment without control. They don't control anything. But I don't think you can have control without discernment.

JoK: Yes!

JK: Yes, I think that's true. But I can tell you, if you've been trained in discernment, achieving control is very much helped.

TC: Absolutely. I think it's necessary to discern. And, you don't have to be consciously aware. When you pick up a cup of coffee or open the refrigerator. You often do things without awareness. A lot of what we do is without awareness, which is part of being human.

JK: I don't do anything like that. What are you talking about?

JoK: Ha, ha. Of course, thinking of things that we're personally involved with, the discernment is of our own states or actions.

JK: Consider the following: Mama says to little Johnny, "Johnny, stop writing on the walls." Johnny hears, discerns, considers his behavior in the past, for example, writing on the walls. He now knows that that behavior would likely be punished or at least not rewarded—it would have consequences. And so, he stops writing on the walls because he discerns that action. So, we're in agreement.

Discernment is essential for learning control. If you think of it in terms of feedback of a mechanical device. The feedback is involved in giving information to the machine. Whether it is to cut back on the amount of gas going through the car, or to increase it. Or to the heater—to increase the temperature, etc. The achievement of control is done by information. It is information that is used in control. Or becomes essential in control. You can't steer a car or a ship without knowing where you're going. And so, that seems to be the heart of it.

I should add, of course, that my interest of discrimination comes from a lot of introspection that I did as a kid and adolescent. Wondering: what the hell was life all about. There were some pretty depressed periods of my adolescence and later on where I often asked what were the important things in life, what was the source of happiness. Strange, I think discrimination training of things along the lines of training for self-information.

Chapter 5

Joe and Joanne Meet

JoK: *We got married in '71.*

JK: *Hey, so what happened in 1971?*

JoK: *We got married.*

JK: *Oh—I didn't know*

JoK: *It was March 7th, Joe. It's 45 years now.*

JoK: We went to dinner. It was friendly. We saw each other the next day, and I found out the previous day was his birthday. He said he didn't tell me because he said he didn't know me well enough. My father was teaching at USC. I told my dad and friends about Joe. They said, "Why are you living here in LA?" Then I moved to San Francisco and Joe found me an apartment.

JoK: We got married in '71.

JK: Hey, so what happened in 1971? JoK: JoK: We got married.

JK: Oh—I didn't know

JoK: It was March 7th, Joe! It's 45 years now.

TC & CK: Wow. OK. Very nice.

JoK: But, as I already said, we met when I was living in Los Angeles. We met at Langley Porter. I was housesitting for some mutual friends, and they said that because I was interested in some things that they thought were similar to what Joe was interested in and that I should call him. And I did. Finally, before they came home because I was embarrassed not do it after they had asked me to do it. I was kind of shy. And so anyway the rest is history, as they say. It was in 1968.

JK: As a 92-year-old, I can tell you the grandchildren and the great grandchildren begin to be a great piece of my life.

TC: Well, tell me: how many children do you have?

JK: I have directly four children at my last count. And then there are six grandchildren. And do we have great grandchildren yet? No, we don't have great grandchildren yet. That should happen fairly soon.

TC: How many grandchildren do you have?

JK: Well we're counting on her fingers right now.

JoK: Six.

JK: So, we have established our genetic map on the face of the earth.

TC: Isn't that wonderful. I imagine they're geographically in different places.

JoK: Well yes, but they tend to cluster around here. The one that just got married is the one that we went to the wedding. He and his new wife live in Brooklyn. But the rest of them are around this area and the youngest ones are just ten minutes away. And the oldest one of those plays chess with his grandfather.

JK: And it's beginning to trouble me, some of these kids are beginning to beat me.

TC: That must be fun. I find that very satisfying when the kids or the grandkids do it better.

JK: Yes, we do have to confess mixed emotions at the end of these games when these guys take me down, but it's really wonderful to be able to play with them; they enjoy the game. They bring their own sets now. And so, I have two or three of them that I can play with. It's great. By the way I'm a little distressed about the fact that it seems to be that boys are much more inclined to get into chess than girls do. Now I'm wondering if that is just due to actual genetic differences between their brains. But I suspect it's mostly good upbringing and the kind of environment in which they grow. What's your hunch on that?

TC: Well, that's a really fascinating question Joe. I tend to believe it's probably a combination of both. Chess is, of course, competitive. And at the end of a chess game you have nothing left but a box of chess pieces. Compared to other activities which might be more either constructive or social.

JK: Certainly, there is that. But there is also the kind of quantitative abstract thinking requirement too—that I suspect is also partially genetic.

TC: Possibly. I'll tell you you're asking me for my opinion and I'm going to give you my opinion. I doubt that females have any less skill in the things needed for chess but I believe there may be less of a sense of motivation or putting importance on it. I'll make an interesting note which I believe is true and that is that men are more likely to get.

JK: Well yes. But I think, my guess is that, there is a correlation between chess and quantitative capacity. Abstract mathematical thinking.

TC: Let me make an observation. I'm told, and I believe it's true, that when learning directions to get somewhere—for example in your car—women are more likely to want to have procedural directions and they don't want to hear about North, South, East, and West. They want to hear, "Go to this place, turn right until you see that, then go this way, and that." And the men tend to want a map to go, "Yeah, it's six miles northeast of here." And you say that to a woman and she's going to say, "What the heck are you talking about? I asked you how to get somewhere." And you said, "It's six miles northeast of here. Why did you change the subject?"

JoK: I would agree with Tom. Certainly, visual cues are very important to women when driving because you also want to know where you go left or right. And also, approximately how far do you want to be. You want the identifying landmark to tell you when to start looking.

And also, in chess and checkers the two youngest have played. The boy, very eager, and very good at it, gets mad at his older sister because she wants to use the chess pieces in a little fantasy of making them do a tea party. But she doesn't want to follow the rules of chess you know.

JK: And that of course is characteristic of those two.

TC: And let me further respond to your comment, Joe. Because I think where we're heading with this is that it's not so much ability as it is inclination to think that something is valuable. So, I mean, I for example, have had occasions where I kind of turned down a chess game because I wasn't interested. I wanted to learn a piece of music or I wanted to go upstairs and make something to eat or something. You know what I'm like. I don't want to sit and play chess and push these pieces around on the board for the next hour. And you know: somebody wins, or somebody loses. I think it's more of interest and putting value on things than native ability.

JK: It's an interesting question. But I think we both agree that a multiplicity of factors is involved in the differences. They're all real and both cultural and genetic components play a heavy role in both.

TC: So, it is very interesting, but I think one thing that does come out highlighted is there are culturally learned biases and lessons and I'm sure that has an enormous amount to do with it.

JK: Yeah sure. Oh yeah. I would imagine that you could find these differences if you go across the world and look at the games that the children play in different countries and where adults play. I'm sure you would find substantial differences. OK, enough of that. So anyway, I want to say to you that I am still thinking that I ought to do the story of my life. I'll tell you—thinking is a lot easier than doing.

TC: And that's what we're transcribing: everything that we talk about. So, if you wanted to talk about some topic please do.

JK: So, I should just talk into a tape recorder?

TC: We're recording right now.

JK: Yeah. That would be the kind of thing that I think perhaps I should cultivate in future because at the present time I'm sort of saying, "Hey, my God, the time is passing." I do want to have some thoughts put down. These are reflections of my life. Certainly, included among those things are the sorts of things that one goes through in adolescence where I felt for a long time I was totally depressed. Joanne reminds me that you are recording for this purpose. So that's OK by me.

Chapter 6
Joe Busy at Work

For example, at certain points of the plug board the signal would be coming from the subject's head, or from the amplifier that amplified the subject's head signal, and that signal could then be directed to a specific further element down the line like a pen that squiggled the exact synchrony with the ups and downs of the voltage.

JK: Meanwhile, *Psychology Today* wrote an article about my alpha biofeedback work. That was in 1968, I believe. The whole thing became quite popular with my colleagues, but also became quite popular with the public and biofeedback grew to become a widely used procedure in psychotherapy and psychiatry.

CK: What did biofeedback look like at that time? Do you recall? What sort of equipment were you using?

JK: It was fairly primitive stuff because it was stuff I parceled together from the different components. For example, the very first one was a standard EEG, which only produced wavy lines on a moving strip chart, often known as the electroencephalogram. Because the pens are activated by a voltage that fluctuates in exactly the same manner as the brain wave, I took the electronic signal and filtered it in such a way as to extract the alpha rhythm, which is about 8-10 Hz or 10 cycles per second, let them hear a tone whenever it appeared in strong enough intensity on the paper and therefore in the electronic tone controller. And that's how the system worked. It was completely put together by whatever things I could grab in the way of sound amplifier, and etc. It was maybe in about three or four years that commercial companies started building that stuff and at the same time, also other types of biofeedback had begun to be popular. For example, people learned how to control their heart rate by getting into different states of mind to produce a tone that would either slow the heart rate or make it more regular. And to perhaps think of exciting things to increase the heart rate.

And then muscle tension became a big thing for people to develop. It turns out that if you put the same type of electrode as the EEG but you put them on, instead, let's say muscles on the head, neck or shoulders, or on the forearms, the slightest amount of tension or muscle activity will be created just simply by thinking about clenching your fist. You don't even have to make a clench. You can think about it and it could actually create the initial muscle activity. And so that system is possible to train people who had headaches that came from excess tension of the muscles around especially the scalp. And what they learned to do was to reduce the intensity of that muscle activity by a sound that reflected how strong the muscle activity was. And so, the person learned to quiet the sound as she lowered the tone as she worked at reducing her muscle tension. The system, called biofeedback, that became popular and is now widely used by thousands of different people and that's it!

So, Joanne said to stop talking.

JoK: No, no! I want to get back to the question about your initial setup in the lab. Was it an old Beckman or Grass device? You had a plug board and a few wires connected to the circuits.

JK: Yeah. That's right. Joanne reminds me of the actual laboratory set up that I used—which looked like a mad man's lab.

CK: Do you have pictures?

JK: I might have. I don't recall bothering to take pictures though. And I think some people came and took pictures. I may have some lying around someplace. If I do, I will show them to you.

JoK: It was a plug-board circuit system that was commercially produced. So, the design is on circuits.

JK: For example, at certain points of the plug board the signal would be coming from the subject's head, or from the amplifier that amplified the subject's head signal, and that signal could then be directed to a specific further element down the line like a pen that squiggled the exact synchrony with the with the ups and downs of the voltage. Or it could be fed to a device that processed the electrical signals so to detect its intensity, or amplitude as we say. The size of the waves could then be monitored, and the board was therefore very useful for doing different experiments because each plug board would be designed to do very specific and different things. And it was what made possible trying out a number of different ideas that one might have explore with biofeedback. So, anyway, it was a lot of fun and I thoroughly enjoyed it. Well what was really great was I was not burdened with a huge teaching load and I was pretty much left to survive on grants that I would get from the National Institute of Mental Health to do this kind of work.

And they kept providing me money to do these studies.

And so, I finished up my career that way and really didn't get myself involved that much in teaching although I did hold a seminar for the medical students at UCSF. And the students in the department of psychology who had just formed about the same time I was there. It had a few Ph.D. students and one or two came to the lab and learned how to do biofeedback and then attend classes in graduate psychology. Mostly, they got their PhDs and carried on in different careers in different places. So that pretty much completes the story.

CK: Tell me about some of the students. Are you in contact with any of them still? Do any of them stand out in terms of their contribution to the research.

JK: Yes. I must confess I haven't been in regular contact with very many of them. There are a few in town. Karen Naifeh is one who is somewhat local and has a private practice in San Francisco. I haven't seen her for at least four or five years, but I consider her a close friend. It's interesting that you mentioned that because I was just thinking about her yesterday. In fact, I looked up her telephone number to give her a call to see how she's doing. She's married to a psychiatrist and they live in San Mateo. There's a guy named Jim Johnston whom you may know.

CK: Yes, I know Jim. He and I are actually in contact now because he wants to write something about you to include in this book.

JoK: Jim actually taught physics in San Diego, but he moved up here to be with Joe at his lab. And he was our really chief computer wizard and programmer and designer of lots of special feedback protocols. And he was able to pull miracles out of the old PDP15. Tom, you may know what that's like. And then he was able to use every last bit and bite on that machine to do what we wanted to try.

JK: Jim is still a close friend. He lives in Berkeley and he came by to visit just the other day. And he asked me about a book that people are writing about me.

CK: Ha, ha—we're working on it right now, Joe. That's what Tom and I are doing all this time.

JK: Honestly, I thought I was talking to Joanne's sister. And I just now realized I'm talking to Cindy. Good God!

JoK: And Tom!

JK: Tom's not on the line. Is he?

TC: Oh! I sure am.

JK: Oh my God! Hey listen! This old man he ain't half there these days and he's clearly getting caught up, I guess. Damn! Anyway, you heard the story. So now you have to just, simply make the proper translations and the story is still true. Now that I'm realizing that I'm talking to sophisticated people about biofeedback, Joanne is completely beside herself by my confession that I had not known.

JoK: I did tell you Joe. But you didn't have your hearing aids on then.

CK: If there's anything you want to change—now that you know it's us—this is the time to do that.

JK: Well I don't need to have hearing aids when I use the telephone. And fortunately, the one phone that I am using is capable of being a loudspeaker at the same time. You don't have to move it up to my ear. Joanne and I can both hear what we're saying in this conversation as I hold the phone about a foot away from my mouth. Anyhow, let me say that the field of biofeedback has, for me, still a lot of promise.

And in my view, it's terrifically important that we are able—by technology—to monitor what is happening in our brains as our brains produce the experiences that we're aware of, so that—in other words discover ourselves through our brains with this technology. And I think that we haven't really explored the potential along those lines. I think for too much the whole field has been dedicated for clinical applications like you know you have tension headaches, OK? You have migraines, OK? That causes checking circulation to the brain. So, you monitor blood flow to the brain.

So, you have insomnia—so you learn how to relax and learn how to produce sleep waves and so on. The clinical applications, of course, are of interest. And they do provide some good reason for a starving scientist-clinician to start creating a little practice of treating patients. And that's what the current professional field of biofeedback is: consisting of a few thousand people who sort of earn their livings at least partially treating patients.

And that technique is now used not only in the States but throughout the world. And it's a very important development for practical reasons.

But I can be accused of being lost in the clouds because what I'm saying is that the human capacity for introspection just sitting and observing what's going on in one's mind.

This is something that is greatly amplified and assisted by the use of technology that monitors the electrical activity of brain insofar as it may be related to the feelings and thought processes that are available through introspection.

So under some visions of the field for the future one might be able to think of public schools training children how to monitor their brain activity as they learn to solve problems and how they are to monitor brain activity as they think about the different phases of their life and miseries and the pleasures that they are experiencing. My point here is that the technology need not be restricted to the treatment of clinical patients in need of assistance to solve certain problems like headaches etc. But it can also be used for self-exploration which is what the human being has that is unique in the whole story of evolution and in creating all of the things that we now call art, science, etc. And I think that we are only at the threshold of what exciting developments might occur in the course of self-discovery when it is aided by technology.

I would hope that sometimes people like Tom Collura and others would begin to encourage this kind of thing in their products and in the publicity about them because I think that everybody ought to own a EEG biofeedback device and it should be done in mass production for a few hundred bucks. I think a very sophisticated piece of hardware could be available to the public and I daresay we would have a slightly more informed human being when we get this kind of thing going then than we are now.

We might be able to detect far sooner than we currently are able to do the kinds of reveries and thoughts or these kinds of slight resentments one might have but not entirely clear; one tries to deny them, but they can pop up in consciousness. That kind of thing I should think would be—could be—detected by electronic means of the EEG. And with much more sophisticated signal processing capacities than we now have. But that's almost a trivial matter these days with today's modern table-top computers and even pocket computers.

CK: I think it's actually gotten over that point and almost concerning because people can buy devices that are being developed by people who really don't understand psychophysiology in the way that they should. But they're creating these devices that people can buy without any clinical, interventional, or relational assimilation. And I think that that is taking what you're saying to too far of an extreme.

JoK: Or maybe in the wrong direction.

JoK: Let's get back to your early time here, Joe—after we were back in the lab. Certainly, you had the smaller lab up at Langley Porter and UCSF kept combining more and more facilities. We moved into an old house on 4th Avenue owned by the university and then moved into another larger house on 5th Avenue when they tore down the 4th Avenue block. I think perhaps to put up a new dental school or something like that. It was on 4th and Parnassus.

JK: One of the wonderful things about this was that I had a whole four- or five-bedroom private residence by the University and I had access to the entire house for my lab. And it was only a block away from the main medical school at UCSF. That was a real break for me because I no longer had to struggle in tiny lab spaces.

JoK: It was very nice, it was spacious. And we were up the street from some other colleagues. Paul Ekman had his lab down the street and he and Joe would confer a lot. They wouldn't combine projects, but they certainly talked to each other a lot.

There were others also. We had a lot of medical students. Very sharp. Very great. I'm thinking of Charlie Weber, Scott May, and others that did go on into biofeedback, that incorporated it into their medical practice.

Things expanded around the Bay Area in various facilities. So, there were a lot of post-docs. It's been a while; I would need to list them. Wonderful memories and lots of fun, too.

TC: A thought that keeps coming up is that all this work that happened in the 1970s, which was interested in gaining some insight into personal growth, of what happened and what seemed to be a very good vision, hope and dream—that it's still waiting to flower and grow and to be profitable to people who write and teach and do therapy now. Joe, people just love your candid and open views of what happened in the 1970s and what may have occurred in the ensuing years until now.

CK: I'm thinking it would take me two hours to respond to that!

JoK: One thing, it got more difficult to get grants in this area. We would live and die by grants at UCSF. Joe had DARPA funding, and private foundation money. People were doing things in private practice, it was kind of like all this stuff was ahead of the curve, if you will. There were many people in the societies. There was a big long struggle to get certification in place, that wasn't there. The intent was for practitioners and medical groups to get certification so they could get reimbursement.

I remember at one of our annual meetings we had US Senator Daniel Inouye speak about becoming recognized as a discipline and become legitimate and get recognized for third party reimbursement—from the VA for example. It was an effort, and it was successful, to position biofeedback research and practice so practitioners could get reimbursed. Also, so practitioners could have a standard of which to follow. That took a lot of effort in the 70s.

CK: Was Joe supportive of certification?

JoK: Yes, he was. He was supportive. He was not doing practice work but wanted the field to be on a solid scientific footing.

Also, there were a few manufacturers that were supportive and were important. Some of the people were a little bit hands-off regarding instrumentation and recommendations. He would talk about the good things people were doing, and, importantly, which things were good to be doing.

There were quite a few who wanted to further the field in the instrumentation area. But others did not want to be bothered with all that. It was an attitude that was there. One of Joe's doctoral and post-doc students shared an office with someone who wanted the equipment removed whenever he used the shared office. He didn't want his clients to see the equipment.

The climate changed, there were more people in a broader base, more published information. But there was pushback from the medical people. Even with all the published data some people still didn't believe it. Barry Sterman got flack. The idea that epilepsy could be modified or cured in some nontraditional way; the medical community didn't believe that was possible.

TC: It was Barry Sterman who got grants terminated. We now know—40 years later—that Barry Sterman probably should have gotten the Nobel Prize because it was efficacious.

JoK: It was shown to be efficacious over and over. But there was a lot of resistance. You know, NFB takes time. Its efficacious but takes time. You just can't swallow a pill. Some people hired people under their supervision, but they were not wholeheartedly involved. It took too much time. It was not cost-efficient maybe? I am not sure what or why. There was a split. Some said it is great. Some said I just don't want to get this on me.

Also, there were other things back then like biorhythms and things using the term "bio-."

When I was on the Board of the Biofeedback Society of California, I was sitting next to someone who said, "Biofeedback in some clinical areas was associated with holistic health and associated with unproven disciplines, the image of biofeedback was associated negatively with that." This was when David French was president in the mid-70s.

There was a guy going around the country talking about healing, no instruments, no training to get into the "alpha level." Joe heard about it. He got a letter from the president of *Psychophysiology* asking, "What is this?" This guy was saying "Joe Kamiya this and Joe Kamiya that." Joe sent a letter saying, "cease and desist." The guy then began boasting, "I am in correspondence with Joe Kamiya." So, you see how this stuff gets going. There were lots of things like that. Very interesting people came through our lab. They were interested in NFB and the states and images that went with the feedback they were getting.

There are lots of things that we never published. There was a group called the New College, a high-quality group, and a class from there wanted to come and participate. They were remarkable. They did alpha training and caught on right away. Every one of them was a quick learner and they all had variations of EEG and yet could change it. They picked up quickly on recognizing their own internal states. Well, we were criticized for only taking the good ones!

CK: That doesn't seem like self-selecting to me.

JoK: There was a lot of interest in meditation. Most people were happy to come. Some people became friends over the long run. They didn't hit Nirvana, but they thought the experience was helpful.

We could not get this past public schools. We were looking at eidetic imagery. There was a lot of interest from meditation groups, Zen groups, a lot of different groups. Some groups worked on getting funding themselves. I remember one researcher, who had recorded group session data, and a guy said, "I need the raw trace of EEG." The researcher said we have not finished analyzing these. And the person said, "I need these for a meeting coming up, someone else is getting $50,000 [in grants] for this." The trend wore out at the same time a much sounder basis was produced. I don't know where they are today.

TC: What is your memory of James Hardt?

JoK: He was convinced alpha was a path to Nirvana. He came to us from Carnegie Mellon; he was a student and in one of our experiments. He was accidently hooked up for longer than should have been. It was my fault, I accidently hooked him up longer than usual and he had a transcendent experience. He was somewhat difficult after that. We tried hard to work with him after that. He was convinced that he could do this for everyone, and it would be best for everyone.

TC: Well he is still working with alpha training. He got Sanjay Gupta hooked up. He is in Vancouver now. I experienced his seven-day training and it was a life-changing experience. I found alpha feedback as profound.

JoK: I did it myself. I found it interesting. But I just would not make the same claims James did.

CK: His behavior can be somewhat incongruent with what he teaches.

JoK: He became more difficult with Joe. He worshipped him, but he was dissapointed when he was not put in charge of the lab at Langley Porter while Joe traveled. He went on to complain to the head of the program.

TC: I think there is a bigger message. Maybe the types of people who are attracted to NFB—at times they are extremes, sometimes arch-conservatives and some very liberal.

CK: Yes, some of the extremists are attracted. I agree. But they are not the average biofeedback practitioner.

TC: I'm thinking about something that Joe said: that there is also an aversion to look at this kind of thing from the average person.

JoK: I guess we are getting on to something: extremes at both ends of the spectrum. In San Francisco, generally, that group as subjects left because there was not enough entertainment value. But three quarters of the people who stayed were great, they learned. By the way, the modalities generalized to other areas.

CK: I don't practice anymore. But I did get more introspective types of people when I did. Marin County, where I practiced, has a lot of people like this—people interested in developing their life long-term.

JoK: The multidisciplinary interest we had in 1969 from academics and lots of other disciplines was just pure interest and curiosity. That is when Barbara Brown was elected as president of the Biofeedback Society. That is where biofeedback term was first coined. Things changed with less grants, which led to less travel for attending conferences; people would go to local meetings only. That was when there was a big focus on certification, which was successful.

Then the pushback from the medical field that didn't believe in this stuff.

JK: The Langley Porter lab was a sound-deadened room, I used it for EEG feedback training alpha rhythms, I taught them to be aware of alpha by a bell when in alpha, when not in alpha, I said "wrong," and they learned.

CK: This was an extension of Chicago work?

JK: Yes, at the University of Chicago I did the first procedure, which was to discriminate alpha. The subjects learned how to identify and discern its presence. And that was the beginning of brainwave biofeedback.

CK: Who did you work with?

JK: I worked at Langley Porter and everyone, five or six of us, had different projects. I was on the committee of ITP, or "Inter-Disciplinary Training." I attended and led a small seminar of interdisciplinary students, 10-20 students, PhDs and others, and I led a seminar.

CK: Do you have pictures? It would be great to include any in the book.

JK: I will look for pictures. I had equipment with wires coming from a person's head. With a pen graph writing out amplitudes of brainwaves. I used a plug-board to design specific things and ideas of measuring. I was not burdened by a large teaching load. NIH provided me with money. I lead a seminar for medical school students and had a few PhD students that I taught biofeedback to. That completes that story.

Chapter 7
The Future

For example, at certain points of the plugboard the signal would be coming from the subject's head, or from the amplifier that amplified the subject's head signal, and that signal could then be directed to a specific further element down the line like a pen that squiggled the exact synchrony with the with the ups and downs of the voltage.

TC: These dialogs provide a view of a future that is transformed by our collective consciousness, and by our individual view of consciousness. A world in which people are no longer classified and vilified by assigning myriad psychiatric and psychological "disorders." A world in which the DSM is viewed as an archaic relic of a primitive view of brain and mind. A world in which individual differences and individual potential are paramount both in personal life and in the social order. A world in which pharmaceutical intervention is seen for the misguided crutch that it often provides, and in which the power of each individual to be optimal and fully self-actualized is a reality.

A world in which even preschoolers understand the vocabulary of the internal world, and are no longer victimized by abuse, trauma, and misunderstanding. The expansions in consciousness and mental health that the participants envision herald significant changes in social justice, multicultural awareness, and the role of individuals as part of a larger collective experience. No longer are people expected to fit into standardized norms, to take prescribed roles, or to change in order to suit global interests. Education has been transformed into a medium of optimal growth and change, and industry is something that serves society, rather than controlling it. The use of pharmaceutical chemicals in pursuit of happiness, peace of mind, and simple mental functioning is a thing of the past. Happiness comes from within, peace of mind is an inalienable endowment, and healthy mental functioning is a sacred right.

The use of technology can transform life, but it can also subvert life. Rather than depending on electronics, chemistry, and physics to bolster and fix our lives, the vision here uses technology to enhance and grow consciousness and awareness, and everyday life with it. Technology used to inform, to educate, to enlighten, to train, and to deliver to freedom, not to deliver to subservience. Too often technology is used to "fix" patients, to "cure" disorders, and thus to subvert the power of the individual to be alive and healthy.

We are only at the threshold of using this technology.

JK: The field of biofeedback has a lot of promise. We are able, by technology, to monitor in our brains; we can discover ourselves through our brains with this technology. We haven't really explored it fully. We have used it for clinical applications, and it provides good reasons to treat patients. The clinical technique is used throughout the world.

I think you have a good point. I think that there's all too much profiteering and new kinds of salvation being peddled with these devices and Americans in particular educated ones these days, often middle-class ones, subject to various kinds of self-improvement programs of modern ring and modern sounds. One is to be very careful that the devices like biofeedback don't fall victim to that type of exploitation. I think it could become self-monitoring by the public. I think it could become self-monitoring though by the public given proper leadership by the people who train others. And it raises an interesting question because I think that, yes it is true, there's a lot of phony baloney can be done for and led by people who are completely uninformed—naïve people who may be well-intentioned but can do as much harm is good In emphasizing the potential for future, I tend to forget that possibility.

There were hints of that sort of thing in the very early stages of biofeedback but fortunately that has faded away. I'm always troubled about the use of the brain wave for the reason that people like to think magical things can be happening. And I made it by myself maybe somewhat subject to my own fantasies about the advantage of the technology of brain monitoring. But I do feel that it is true that a vast area of technologically-aided introspection can help all of us be clearer about what we're thinking, about who we are or what we're trying to be, and how we feel about ourselves.

I had been thinking about a conversation that has led me to believe that it would be very important to try to engage many others in our field and in related fields to talk about the importance of the basic concept of relating our everyday experiences, opinions, emotions, feelings sensations, thoughts, and memories to the biological substrate on which you operate. And to expand, therefore, knowledge of 'human' or the human condition. And knowing from whence we came, evolutionarily, of course. But also, where we might be able to advance our knowledge by knowing more than we now know about the relation between these psychological things and the neurophysiological and physiological things. And it would seem to me that getting this area started would be one of the best things that psychophysiology and feedback could accomplish for the future. And it seems to me that there are plenty of talented people who, especially perhaps, in the neurophysiology area, but in other areas too, who can expand our range of knowledge of things that are happening in brain and body at the same time.

We are experiencing our subjective things that are mentioned. Anyway, that's the one thing that I thought about since last speaking with you because I feel that this field of, let's call it psychophysiology or biofeedback-aided psychophysiology or biofeedback-aided self-knowledge—or whatever it is. This area, I believe is going to be the hot model for all the future among the sciences. And, I think that it would be very useful for us to try to engage more people in contributing their work and their conceptions into this area.

So that's my little affirment for the day.

CK: Do you have any people in mind?

JK: Oh. Well! I know somebody, including the two I'm speaking to right now. And of course, there are many in the field of psychophysiology. I think—the two of you though. Because you have had so much experience talking with others and in relation to your organization you have a lot of experience in that area.

I would be willing, if it would be of any value, to try to jot down the names of some people I think would be useful, but I would want to give some thought to the process before I could name anybody right now. You know it's an area where I think we need to stimulate a lot of thinking along scientific lines as opposed to purely therapeutic lines. While therapy is a tremendously important practical term of psychophysiology and biofeedback. But it should not be, in my view, used only for the advancement of therapies or what we call re-education. Re-education in the sense of what I've been earlier speaking of, yes; it could be really very useful.

It is a tremendously exciting area when you think about the fact that we humans are evolving into people who are developing instruments of knowledge that further our evolution in specific directions. Our evolution is not just a passive force of survival of the fittest but very much a path of active participants attempting to control it! That's what we are doing.

The field of biofeedback has been helpful in that regard, although it has focused on the cure of ailments, of one kind or another, especially the psychosomatic type. But biofeedback is a tremendous tool for self-exploration of one's own entire central nervous system to the extent that we can monitor it with EEG and with our various physiologic monitors. Increasingly, as we become more sophisticated in about what both central and peripheral nervous systems are doing in our daily lives and sophisticated in monitoring the EEG and other physiologic measures associated with these things.

We are in for new discovery of ourselves in ways that have not been available. In the past if we didn't feel well, we used a thermometer—stuck in the mouth that could tell us why that was so. We haven't gone too much farther in developing physiologic monitors of our states of mind but, I think our field has a unique opportunity to excel in and to show the world some of the things that can be done now. We can use the biofeedback devices to pioneer the scientific development and exploration of the human mind. It is exciting and goes way beyond the treatment of specific ailments.

That is my central philosophy and faith in this field. I think it points to an exciting new era as our technology becomes more and more sophisticated, especially in monitoring brain and autonomic functions. We are in for some bright days going into the future. I am happy that I have been able to be a part of it and I think that it won't be too long before the educational systems of our country realize it will be worthwhile to teach kids to monitor their own muscle tensions, brainwaves, and autonomic arousals as they relate to their moods, angers, pleasures, and their sense of happiness. I think once people use these tools for self-improvement, self-development, or self-education, the field will become increasingly more widely recognized as a fundamental development in human civilization.

TC: That is a noble vision, Joe, thank you for that.

JK: I don't think the world is yet fully aware of the tremendous value of this as an educational tool. I would predict that if the public education system got smart, they would start teaching kids, besides the physical education—exercises outdoors, they would give them a good set of experiences with biofeedback, learning how to change their muscle tensions and learning how to change their pulse rate and things like that. Self-mastery of their own processes which really requires self-understanding about how one's brain and body works in relation to one's moods and so on. We have tended to emphasize control, control, control. But, when you think about the control of any behavior, whether it be internal or external, it always implies feedback of information to make that control possible.

But anyway, it's a kind of a thing that is sort-of a, certainly, elusive quality. But because, even as I speak of what it was that I was excited about and was just reminded of in what you just said so it slipped off again.

Anyway, this is an interesting cognitive problem for me right at the moment. I'm a little embarrassed to be admitting it. But if I try now, then let me just say whether I can now recall you guys are good therapists you can perhaps recall what it was that I was getting into when we were talking and I got thinking that we could do much better in training our children and in the public school system to use technology of the EEG and other forms of neuro- and bio-feedback as sort of a branch of physical education. And it would be I think, I know, that children would be interested in doing it because with Joanne's experience in giving biofeedback to elementary school children, they really got very interested. Let's see, I think that was maybe even preschool. Anyway, it was, in any case, really kind of an intriguing piece of news that she came home with that these kids were really very, very interested. They couldn't wait to get their turns to being hooked up with GSR or EEG or both. But they were all just very much alert because, I guess, the appeal was, "Hey! this is something about them which is you know far more interesting than anything out of a comic book or whatever history or whatever else they might be asked to read in school. And so I think that I got both of you agree that this would be a good thing to introduce into the public school system, simple exercises in, for example GSR, and tell that child to think of some bad word that he is not supposed to use (he doesn't have to say it.) All they'll have to do, is to sort of say it to themselves and there should show a GSR response that's quite more marked than something like merely pronouncing his name, or saying his street address, or whatever.

There's always some arousal that occurs just from the simple fact of speaking. But the simple fact of speaking certain things, like for instance, maybe the child might learn the word shit or f. . . or something like that that would trip it because he is being punished for it and has been sternly told by his parents that he must not say such things. So that would be a kind of self-discovery of his own autonomic nervous system and that's the kind of thing that I was talking about last time and you helped me to recapture it again this morning.

The discernment, the discrimination, and if you will in older terms, the introspective acuity that is involved in this, is a tremendously important thing to be developing. I think that in the future, kids who are in the 6th grade will be writing essays on their experience with EEG or other kinds of biofeedback.

TC: Yes.

JK: The manufacturing can be such that it can be reasonably marketed at a lower price, so everyone has access to it.

TC: That's quite a vision. To continue this thinking: If you look at things like rocket ships and space exploration and science, space exploration, and rocket ships, and now we have walked on the moon and we are talking about sending our grandchildren to Mars. Many people think that that exploration is critical to the survival of humanity. That at some time in the distant future our destiny is that we will be among the various planets and even stars or what have you. I am interested in using that analogy for inner space exploration. What is the vision of what we can become through our exploration of inner space?

JK: Yes, that's wonderful. I think in very concrete ways too, for those who like to see the applied for improvement can certainly, I think, help in the development of close relationships between people since we have evolved as social creatures and our physiology has been to a great extent shaped by the fact of our social interactions and symbolic interaction processes. We can be sure that in the future if we hook ourselves up with other people at the same time, those that we live with, our children or our parents, mates or so on, I think we can learn a lot about the interaction of ego development and the development of the person's self-image as a social creature. This, I think, can go a long ways if developed properly and I believe it could become a great commercial success if properly advertised. I have a hunch that it would be a tremendous thing to have in public schools—certainly parts of the day or certain days of the week can be devoted to using biofeedback devices. It would be almost as important as crayons, and writing paper, etc., as a tool of education. Now we have biofeedback devices which are a tremendous advance into the discovery of the internal world of the organism. This tool tunes into the internal world of the child. That is my vision for the future, and I don't think I am too far off, actually.

TC: That is an interesting insight. Currently, there is talk of neurofeedback in the political arena because one of the candidates for the cabinet is very interested in neurofeedback. It becomes controversial because of the politicization of the whole process; neurofeedback itself comes under their scrutiny. There are those that have a political aim one way or the other. I agree, it would be a terrific possibility if it would happen.

JoK: Can you say a little more about that, Tom?

TC: Well sure, if you are interested... The candidate is Betsy DeVos and she actually is active in education, particularly alternative and charter education. For better or worse. But she also is an investor in a company which has commercialized neurofeedback and has opened basically storefront outlets where kids can come in and get biofeedback and neurofeedback.

JoK: Sort of like Sylvan Learning Centers and stuff like that?

TC: Very much like that. Very much like that model, yes. And you won't have any trouble finding lots and lots of material on it. You just look for her name Betsy DeVos and then simply type the word neurofeedback. All these things will come up. We have a mixed sense about it. The company itself is certainly not among the worst of those who hype it and try and sell it. They are being criticized because they claim to be able to help so many disorders.

JoK: You know, yes. That's when one starts to feel uncomfortable because of the over-hyping or the exaggerated claim. And that comes from the founders of that particular company. It's OK to do a fee for service. But, you know, I hear that they're claiming to cure all working-world ills with it and that's kind-of off-putting.

TC: So, it's going to be an interesting future that's for sure. One of the things maybe Joe or you could comment on: You know I got into this field in earnest in 1995. Although I'd been in EEG for 20 years and I am continually impressed by the pushback that we get. And one of the areas in which we get pushback I think is the area of "taboo." There are people who say I don't want to know what my brain is doing. And then they make jokes and say, "Oh, if you hook mine up you won't find anything." What is this taboo that it turns people away from going inside and being aware of themselves? Do you have any sense of that? Has the field not grown as much as you or I would have dreamed over the last 40 years? Where is the resistance coming from? That deep sort of resistance—not political, not economic but just a deep resistance of being self-aware?

JoK: People will go to almost any length to not be aware. There is that. Yes, I'm reminded once there was a young kid who was coming to pick up his friend from the lab—back in the old days, and the friend was a volunteer subject. This kid was from somewhere in the South—a very young guy. He was not very sophisticated, he said "What do ya'll do here?" And so, I described what the experiment was and what his friend was doing. And he looked at me, and with each glance was more puzzled and he finally said, "Why would anybody want to do a thing like that?" I think it was unfamiliarity. But the idea was that knowing anything about yourself was foreign. And then there's the people who say it's going to "show them up." You know—the people who are paranoid that they're going to get there, you're going to record them, and then somehow the government's going to get a hold of it. All kinds of stuff like that. You know—paranoid fantasies are going to control their brain. These are the same people who will never go to the doctor because they don't want to know.

TC: I do understand. Yes. And they'll just let things go on and possibly part of it is the feeling that no one can do much about it. If I have a kidney problem, or you know a physical problem, I have some confidence that the medical profession might be able to help me. I think a lot of people feel that if there's anything mental going on they don't trust the medical profession to make a judgment about them and help them. They might just be labeled or vilified. I think that's an important possibility they just don't trust that our science is worthy of it.

JoK: And there is a lack of trust, which touches a broad spectrum of concerns. You know I mean the lack of trust feeds into a lot of things like that.

TC: Correct. So, these are interesting points, and these are things that we all need to think about addressing and hope possibly overcoming if we're going to have a positive vision for mental health.

JoK: This is true for biofeedback of all sorts. It carries over into self-awareness on many levels. So, if people don't want that, then that's certainly something to think about.

TC: Yeah, I agree with you. One thing that I had once thought of and recently put in an article is the idea that there will be an elitism. In as much as the way, you know, certain people will have all the money. There will be certain people who will have all the brain awareness or all of another brain feature.

For what good it is—it certainly won't make people necessarily rich or anything, but I think there will be a group that tends to be more aware and connected to these things.

JoK: And yes, it is true that some people are more aware than others. They've had the education and life experiences—whatever. And there are also fundamentalists, of every sort, all over the place. Anyway, yes, I think it's good to think about all that.

JoK: Let's talk about what experience I've had in the public schools. Students have had success, but how it gets introduced is important. Somebody in the school has to be an advocate. When you go away, it goes away.

TC: Yes. And they have to have a reason. One of my experiences is that the school counselors and principals and such do not think it is at all their job to help treat and cure the kids. They are there to provide an education. It is not their problem if the child has a disorder.

JoK: And by the way, many districts do not want a diagnosis of a disorder even if it is absolutely accurate and true that is one more kid they have to provide for, and it is about money.

TC: Yes.

JoK: Recently, a researcher at UCSF offered to screen all of the kids in the elementary schools in San Francisco for free and the school district turned her down.

TC: Really?

JoK: My experience with teachers was they were quite interested when I presented the idea. But what they wanted first was to have this for themselves. They wanted workshops for them. They were not particularly interested in doing it for the kids at first. They thought it would be fine, but what they really wanted was it for themselves.

TC: Isn't that interesting?

JoK: Yep. That was interesting to me too.

JK: Well, that points to a very important thing and that is that there is a universal curiosity in human beings about themselves. I think that it is a real challenge to feed on that, and to, frankly, develop a commercial product that helps people to look at themselves if they want to. In this context, the term "Mind Mirror" did a good service because that is exactly what a good neurofeedback device will do.

The future, I think, will be quite challenging and interesting to develop by simple examples and so on and staying away from the wild claims that sometimes people make about biofeedback. I may have contributed to the over-enthusiasm about alpha feedback. I think that over-enthusiasm is one of the traits of human beings that will always be with us and we just need to be a little more careful not to cultivate it in others, but at the same time to give the immediate benefits of self-knowledge to other people. I think Joanne pointing out that these people wanted to do it for themselves is a good case in point.

People initially, if they have been told it will reveal some disease, they naturally will want to shy away from it, but if told they may find out some new things about themselves it will increase their confidence in what they know about themselves, etc., then it can really take off. When we think about it, it is really just another important advance in educational practice. It will be successful to the extent that it is presented that way. As opposed to some kind of cure for specific ailments, which is a very limited application. It is very useful for that particular application, but for the general education of a person I think it is a tremendous tool.

TC: Yes.

JK: I am very glad that you, in particular, are interested in these subjects, because you, Tom, know the business end of this biofeedback. I am glad you are involved in this. It seems to me like a challenge of how to market it.

TC: We have done this for some time. The best for us is to present evidence-based results. In business, you turn to where you can. We are going back to talking about personal exploration. I am reading all the early 1970s work. We moved to presenting the scientific results, but I find myself going back to early roots as well.

JoK: Small groups of students, a small medical practice, that can be as effective as trying to develop major state curricula programs.

JK: You know we learn social studies and such in small groups. In our process of interaction in groups we learn a lot about ourselves. But we can learn in small groups in school, churches, in Boy Scouts, Girl Scouts, etc. . . I think people will learn about this as an important tool.

JoK: I was just thinking about having a neurofeedback merit badge!

TC: Yes, a psychophysiology merit badge, that would be great. Let's talk about some future thinking.

JK: It's always fun to speculate about the field because even the ordinary man in the street with no education at all is always interested in how his body and brain work—especially the brain in relation to his total subjective experiences. This includes his pain and his very thought patterns and thinking processes themselves. And so, I must confess I am no particular expert in the analysis of my own experience, but I probably am sort of like a lot of people in that I'm certainly familiar with the major emotions and the general things like thought and confusion and clarity, etc. that people talk about it. It is true that some- times I feel kind of confused especially so when I'm listening to programs because my hearing is slightly defective. I often don't understand what was being said and I get confused and sometimes I just say, "Oh! Screw it. I'm not going to try listening anymore."

This has happened a little bit more of recent than before. There is a slow deterioration of my hearing which annoys the hell out of my wife. Because if she wants to say something, I have to ask her, "What was it you said?" So, it introduces a complicating factor in personal relations because the person may now begin to figure that she must always talk out loud to be heard in most circumstances. However, it's not talking out loud that is the issue but rather catching my attention or knowing that I am oriented toward hearing (or for anybody else). I just went through this morning after chewing my wife out and she said, "Oh forget it." Probably a direction pattern. There is a slow deterioration of my hearing, but it is also a universal problem. It introduces a complicated factor into interpersonal relations.

TC: What you're experiencing is generally true of everyone, in that to a greater or lesser extent, none of us actually hear each other. And that when we try to explain our internal world, the question that pops into my mind is: when do we simply give up, and think that we already know enough? But we really don't and how many counselors spend so much time saying, "Listen to what she is saying; listen to what he is saying." And I think in general we all eventually say, "Oh, forget it." And I think we know enough but we never know enough. So, I'm going to ask you Joe: what would be different if we could actually convey in the language how we feel and what is going on inside of us, instead of the approximation that we live with?

JK: Well, that is the questionable time and it is one that I think all of us can work on to some degree and that's why there's some hope for the technology of amplification. And I think also, probably a little bit of education of people with hearing losses of their partners that would remove a lot of the everyday strife that occurs. And this is particularly relevant to people, who like myself, are in his 90s. There is a gradual hearing loss and it begins to be, at least, a minor irritant in our personal relationship. So anyway, let's do the social psychology of hearing loss. It is an interesting thing that I suspect it's almost universal among good people.

TC: Joe, you're experiencing some physical hearing loss and the way we help you with that, among other things, is either to have you get a hearing aid, or you maybe learn to lip read a little bit. And to have people talk to you directly while you see them and maybe speak more slowly. OK? So, these are all personal aids to hearing what you said. Let me challenge now: what can you imagine in terms of aids to help me hear what you meant? So, I can imagine a machine that makes your voice louder or something so I can hear you but really this critical question is can I hear what it is you're really meaning to say. Can I amplify my understanding or amplify my compassion? Or amplify my vocabulary so that when I hear you, I hear what you mean? And what would that mean for society if people really heard what they mean?

JK: Well that would be a dramatic difference certainly in the daily contact between members of the family, children, and between people of the different generations. It would be a remarkable thing. To me, one may have to be more polite in general, especially regarding those with hearing loss. One can ask, did you understand? It might reduce the negative effects.

Between members of the family, of children speaking to people of the different generations. It would be a remarkable thing. And to me, to get beyond the technology of amplification of sound and improvement of hearing abilities by hearing aids and the like. At the moment I can't see anything, other than to learn, to be, shall I say, just simply more polite in general in relation to people with hearing loss and not just blame oneself for not having heard clearly what somebody else said or being tolerant when somebody else who has a hearing handicap seems to have comprehended what you said and learning the patience that is required to correct the momentary situation to the extent that it is possible.

So, some such questions as, "Did you understand?" or etc. would help in the personal interaction process because it would then keep the negativity, the exasperation, the disappointment that confuses the thinking processes. And, actually the situation between Joanne and me is a good case in point. We are struggling to learn how best to handle this problem of hearing loss. We're learning how to handle it. I've tried my best to call my frustration and anger when I hear her say, "Oh, forget it." So, I suppose a public discussion of the matter is about the knowledge of good people who are professionals in this field of interpersonal counseling. They would be better equipped if they learned some of the problems that the hearing-deficient people have and the problems they have. So anyway, I think this is an interesting field that deserves some attention. And I think it's particularly so as people reach their middle ages and then get on to older. Like myself: the 80s, 90s, 100, even. That would help.

Perhaps the experienced therapists have already known about all these matters and its old hat—I just don't know.

TC: I think therapists struggle with these matters. I don't think they necessarily know the answers. And let me give one example: right now, you are acutely aware of your change in hearing. And so, you are able to say I am right now not hearing as well as I know I could. But what if you never heard any better. And that's all you ever knew. Then you go around thinking that having people, you know, having to speak loudly and having to go through the effort. You'd think that was normal. There's nothing new.

So, let's get back to this idea of being able to actually hear what a person means and to listen properly. I'm going to suggest that many people never learn to listen properly and they don't know that they're not hearing what I mean. And this is where your thoughts can become so interesting. Because we're talking about communicating the internal human experience in a way that the other person actually understands what you mean.

JK: This certainly is a very important area for everybody to learn especially as they go into middle age and then beyond. Because it will certainly help improve the quality of interpersonal relationships and certainly in the areas of professional management of employees, etc. Personnel departments all over the world should become cognitive of the difficulties of this sort of thing and seminars and conferences would do great things to help a lot of people in management where there's a hearing problem.

The issue is one major problem can be solved with hearing aid. However, there's quite a bit beyond just the physical hearing capacity that is the issue. The other matters are to show the capacity to analyze sounds and to hear correctly. People can probably know how to do that very much like maybe a child learns to speak a foreign language. Yes. So, these are interesting topics.

I would like to tell you something that I thought would be worth talking about that does not have to do with what we're now talking about. I discovered a word that I use that is important and that is to ponder. I noticed the other day that I often decide what it is I'm going to do tomorrow or what remains undone today and the conflicts of the world and the conflict I have, etc. I suppose that there it's an aspect of meditation that I'm talking about even though I don't do formal meditation. That is to just sit quietly and ponder where you are, what you are trying to do and how important that is to you. It sounds like one could learn to develop a search mode that inquiries into the matters that are most important in your life. In my case, I thought, "Hey OK—let me just spend a few moments just being quiet and seeing what it is that is running through my mind. What is it that comes to my mind as I sit quietly?"

This is an interesting exercise and I suppose it is complementary among meditation traditions especially the Zen tradition in which one maintains a kind of open alertness to whatever experience comes to him. Just observe it and try not to resolve or judge it—just simply experience it or something like that. I cannot clearly articulate what this experience is. But I've felt that I'm going to do more of it because I think it is going to be helpful to me to sort of, shall I say, keep one's equanimity—one's freshness to his experience? Something like that. I just think it's an interesting thing and I'm sure this emerges partly as the fact that I am 91-years-old and I'm asking a question at several different layers of contemplation. What is it that I want to do with my life? It's a question that has some importance to me and it grows as I get older.

Because I know that statistics say that I'm already past life expectancy probably in the American population and that even though I don't feel at all old in any sense other than a few aches and joints and so on. Nevertheless, I feel that I should know a little bit more of what it is about how I want to orient myself toward the rest of life and certainly maintaining one's calmness and happiness, pleasure in being alive are important points to maintain and even to think about them too. OK, so that would really give me extreme satisfaction with life. These are things worth thinking about and I believe it's certainly worth getting everybody to think about it. And, it becomes more and more important and valuable and helpful to people, especially as they get past middle age.

So anyhow that was one thought that I have had. I cannot say that I am any clearer about what it is that I really want to do "with the rest of my life." But I do think it's the kind of thing that it's really worth hearing and talking about with people and saying, you know, "What do you want to do, Tom Collura, with the rest of your life?"

TC: Well that's a really, really good question. One of my answers is rather of a Zen note in that I really still never know what it is I want to do. I really don't know what my path is. But what I do know is when I'm not on it. There's this feeling, this yearning, this negativity, this sense that—no you're not on it. But then as I move and monkey around and do different things and fall into things, there are things that do give me a sense, both immediately and as I look back on them, and say, "This was a good idea, this was a good decision."

But I do have to say, Joe, and this is what's important to our meetings, our talks, is that you really don't know what the future will look like. And so, you can't say I'm going to get to Point B because you don't know what point B is and you've never seen it.

So, I like having our discussions go in the direction of what things could be like if certain things became possible. And I think that one of the key kernels of what we're talking about is how could it become possible for me to truly understand your internal world. And for you to understand my internal world. And to say that at this point in terms of our ability to communicate that, we are actually deaf. We hear but we don't listen. And it's as if we're talking about temperature and how hot something is but we've never had a thermometer. And now, what if we have a thermometer and what we've learned in history is if we have a thermometer, we can have thermodynamics we can have physics, we have chemistry, and we can fly people around the moon.

And I want to encourage you Joe at your advanced stage. One good reason you have to really look forward to continuing your journey on Earth here is that within a couple of years we will be flying more people out into outer space and while they do that I want to work with you to be exploring inner space.

JK: Yeah, that's actually well put. I'm thinking that one of the things that our culture needs and would be helpful for is for the encouragement of the kind of talk we're engaged in now to be encouraged among people now to discover who we are, what our aspirations really are. And, why? And so on. It just makes life richer and I believe the more lived rather than just simply going through just routine kinds of things. One gets more juice out of life when one does that. These are matters that I think are vitally important and somehow or other, you know, it would be very helpful if those of us who are familiar with the technology for self-monitoring of one's brain and body processes would actually begin to point out that the exploration of what's happening inside the brain and body could be of great assistance along the lines of what we're talking about.

TC: Well you know every little thing has a more global cosmic significance doesn't it. And even something as trivial as brake lights. You're conveying to the other drivers what your intentions are. And you're sharing with them what it is you're doing or not doing. How critical that is!

JK: Yeah. It's a nice example of how the human social nature is capable of being explored and developed experientially. Even with such a simple thing as a brake. It lets people know where you are and what your intention is—certainly with turn signals. It's absolutely crucial. And finally, it's a very interesting analogy that if we had the equivalent in many of the other interaction patterns that we have with people. That if we could express our appreciation of other people. We've gotten pretty good you and I, I think largely in expressing gratitude for somebody else's gift or contribution, whether it's in word, we have learned to interpret and understand signals that we use to communicate our internal state. Then we have all kinds of brake lights and turn signals and warning things that we have learned to use in our everyday lives. And I think it's a continual growing process especially for exploring what we're currently exploring: the world of objective experience. I think it's really worth the price of living, the cost of living, to learn how to understand the inner world as a person and as yourself.

And we have certainly come a long way since we've been chimpanzees in the process of evolution and how we'll get along these lines in the future remains to be seen. But I'm kind of optimistic that the technology of observation of the correlate physiological material process is in association with experience—probably experience in consciousness.

It is a great thing of the future. You know, I believe you sir, are a purveyor of the instrument that can go a long way to advance humankind in understanding what our situation here on earth is.

TC: Yes. And that is our vision of course.

JK: Yeah and I'm really glad you're in that field.

TC: Well I am too and it's a privilege to be able to speak with others because as an instrument provider, I consider our role rather like that of someone who creates musical instruments. And then the performers, the virtuosos, and the composers create, really, the art. And what is gratifying is when the use of the instrument goes beyond what the instrument provider would have imagined.

JK: Yeah, that's right. Yes. And that's what's exciting about our field, I think. What you and I are talking about ought to become a fairly common thing or activity among those who know biofeedback or want to learn biofeedback and neurofeedback it would greatly amplify our appreciation of life. I believe that we can tap into its material base that happens to have evolved along with our experience. In a way I can say that this is probably the sensitive portent instrument in education.

I've mentioned before that teaching children to attend to the body- and brain-processes will help them achieve that richer life. I hope that before too long actual words along these lines can be incorporated in commercial advertisements or the feedback instrumentation that can be made available by manufacturers and surveyors like you. I think that it would be a tremendously important step in human civilization. You are promoting in the sales and manufacture and distribution and training of people in this technology, correlating one's experience with the rest of that process of experience.

TC: I agree Joe. I think it's one of the few things that cannot help—but benefit.

JK: And the problem I ran into: I rather began to, maybe, encourage too much premature thinking of learning how to control alpha as the door into the wonders of life never before experienced, etc. People got kind of pissed off because while I wasn't intentional, I suspect I fostered with the *Psychology Today* message, which was just too popularizing and too much crazy—too much pie in the sky, wishful thinking kind of thing. And that fortunately has died down because people have learned not to make extravagant claims and as enthusiastic, as I would say privately, about the future of neurofeedback, as I ever have been. I think our technology has a long ways to go yet. We have to learn to extract all of our total brain activity in ways that are related to our experience that will make what we currently have rather primitive. I'm hoping that some of the people that you're associated with in everyday life in commerce with EEG will begin to encourage them to, what shall I call it: the phenomenology of life through technology. You know it's something that all of us, when you think about it, are constantly striving to improve upon the total quality or our state of mind and to overcome the challenges and so on. Keeping away negative things, especially depression. I actually think that it will be an instrument of the future that will be very much appreciated. And people say Mr. Tom Collura and Joe Kamiya were people who were saying these things early in the world and should receive Nobel prizes for doing so.

TC: Well whatever! Let me respond to that. First of all, I'll make a comment that personally I would be very happy to be one of those scientists who doesn't really get recognized because some of the most important work was done by people you never heard of. They worked quietly and diligently and that to me gives me my sense of path.

But let me give you a historic perspective of the 1600s and 1700s: there was something called alchemy. And these scientists, if you will, had crude tools they could measure with, and they could weigh things and they had heat. And they knew how to mix things and they thought they were going to turn lead into gold. And, as we know that never happened exactly the way they said. So, there is your pie in the sky. Too much, too early, to claim you're going to turn lead into gold. But wind forward another hundred years or another 200 years. Those same tools improved because the alchemists gave us weighing and the rudiments of chemistry and the concept of observation but then by adding more scientific rigor we had chemistry and then we had physics and the things we can do go way beyond the original promise which was turning lead into gold and have gotten into things such as computers, pharmaceuticals, and space travel. So when we talk further Joe, I want to encourage you to pretend that you were an alchemist in the 17th century but you are going to foresee the chemistry and physics of the brain and mind as it will be in a hundred years or maybe 200 years.

JK: That's great. That's a wonderful challenge because I think you're pointing to some very rich fields of development of human knowledge about ourselves. I am so glad that, at least one person who is in the business of advancing the sale of technology along these lines is around to share these thoughts with me. I think it would be totally interesting to see if other people are interested in this kind of talk that we're engaged. I'm a little bit worried about them because there are so many ego-enhancing processes that get tangled up with this. And, one has to constantly fight off self-enhancement profitable elevation of status kind of thing, among others. It's a very tricky field but I do feel that you and I have inadvertently entered into the discussion of things that are absolutely crucial to the future of our field. And people will be able to say that we should record these conversations.

And hey, I'm sure your colleague and my colleague, who has been in on these conversations, Cynthia, will be recognized as one of the pioneers in the field and I'm very grateful to you for the call because it has really stimulated my thinking along these lines because there's much to do about it. Now, I also feel that I'd like to know if I could contribute any thinking to what your hopes are for what you were doing.

CK: Thanks, Joe.

TC: Oh absolutely.

JK: This is a field that is rich in exploring human consciousness, using new techniques of recording and reinforcing EEG. There is a lot of unrealized potential in this field. We all may have more potential to explore inner consciousness, yet our ego gets in the way.

That's been true from the very beginning. I felt this was beginning to look like science into human consciousness and I still believe that it is a field that is really quite potentially rich with the improved technology—both the handling of the EEG signal and the conditions of reinforcement, etc. As well as the kind of—let's see I've lost my track on that one so let's forget that for the moment.

I do feel that this field has still a lot of unrealized potential. I have the feeling that each of us can learn and have the potential to learn more about what's happening in our brains than we thought possible. I believe it is correct that we have developed various protective attitudes to enhance our egos and keep us from getting too depressed about things or alarmed or whatever. I have the following kind of fantasy, if you will. And I believe it is based on what the potential of this field really is. And that is that a child should become much more familiar about his own brain activity and that makes him mad or he can do to bring his anger down when he's disciplined by his parents or spat upon by his peers. I think that children and all of us, of course, need to realize that all of our emotions all of our experience is a function of our central nervous systems and our autonomic nervous system and the whole damn body that goes with it. We live in a world of our own creation and that subjective world can and should be greatly sharpened in relationship to what's going on in body and brain. And I would think that a serious attempt made by teachers in the education world to try developing this in children, and seeing what happens with the related behaviors such as their social interactions, their IQs, their imaginativeness in story writing, etc. It's a field that is ripe for research and I have the feeling that the more one learns about one's attitudes and forces and their manifestations, I think the better off we are.

I am more shocked this realization—or this view, has not been encouraged much by those who are doing biofeedback. They tended to use this to help the disabled, people who come to them and pay them to help them remove some of their sufferings. But its potential use in the educational domain is, I think, tremendously vast, and why it's not being picked up that way is a puzzle to me.

JoK: Having worked with a few kids with biofeedback, just as an exploratory kind of adventure for them let's say, I found them really interested and they also tended to learn about themselves. They learned, I remember one, had a big run of theta, and I asked, "What was that," and he said, "I'm not telling." I think for me one of the important things—besides just kids learning about themselves, is I feel that it encourages development of the observing self.

JK: I endorse that comment fully, and the development of the observing self is very similar to the notion of the Buddhist concept of self-awareness, and they are really, I think, twin brothers. And I would hope that maybe somewhere the meditation world, which I'm not at all familiar with, as people begin to explore this and write about it, and encourage other people to do so, I'm quite sure that it would be well received by people, in my own experience, people like Tarthang Thulku of the Tibetan Center, and another guy who is an American, and developers of the meditation of the Buddhist sort.

TC: Alan Watts is one.

JK: He was also intrigued, and there were potentially great things, but he was also very apprehensive too, I noticed that perhaps we would begin to pray, and place too much worshipping upon our material selves, as opposed to what he believed, that was more the spiritual world. I think, if I'm wandering, stop me, but I think this area of self-enlightenment, self-awareness, is a legitimate field, and it's one that all of us could gain a hell of a lot more from doing things like EEG biofeedback. Not necessarily alpha, but for God's sake, look at alpha and its relationship to all parts of the brain, other EEG patterns—the whole EEG using 30 or so electrodes. It is an awesome thing to ponder when you think about the fact that a good many of those experiences are potentially capable of being brought to consciousness, through a kind of EEG training. I have the feeling that it would be extraordinarily exciting and a new path for human development. If this could be pushed more, and encouraged by the government, and by individuals. Anyway, I am the optimist, and I just hope that people like you can write up this area and talk it up and get people intrigued and interested in it because I think it's a tremendously challenging field. And we're in a position to be able to help the world discover a lot about itself.

CK: I couldn't agree about that more.

This makes me think about the Chicago experiments because they were innovative in this way – introspectively and subjectively. I heard that you had Elmer Green at Chicago.

JK: Yes. We had Elmer Green to the lab, and he was very interested. He was able to show some remarkable things with yogis. We spoke to him recently.

JoK: He was well when I talked with him. He was 99. He was an important person in this field. We'd met him at the Biofeedback Research Society meetings or ones at Esalen. He has an interesting story about how he came to Menninger, because he saw the building in a vision and drove out there, he was quite interested to tell about that, and he did a lot of things about creativity, and certainly the recording of Yogi Swami Rama and some others from India. One or two came here and worked with Elmer and Alyce—and others.

JK: He certainly was an important person in this field. He was helpful in preventing the over-behavioristic emasculation of the field. To think of it as purely in terms of what you can control and what it can do for specific ailments is very limiting. I hope that the concept of biofeedback, in general, and EEG biofeedback, in particular, should always be promoted not just as a cure for ailments, but as an advancement tool of human intellect and human emotion and human awareness.

You know, you probably know you've pretty much scanned the depths of my soul. You may be able to dig up some more—if I have any great insight, I'll let you know.

What am pondering today is what is this field called biofeedback? And what are we doing in it? And it is true that people have made a very useful thing of it? Such that they can partially make their livings with it. It's a practical device to help people overcome various disorders of mind or body and what is going on in real time. I am however of the mind that the biggest contribution that is yet to be realized from research is how human consciousness is related to this activity that we call biofeedback and how biofeedback can explore that. It's a very intriguing question which calls for a lot of speculation and other things. I must confess I don't have any profound thoughts on the matter except to say that I think that thought as a science, as opposed to just direct applications for the correction of one or more clinical entities, there will be some, I think, pretty substantial rewards. I suspect it emerges from the fact that we are a highly social species and that we are used to labeling our private experiences to get along with each other and to explore and to understand ourselves as a matter of fact too. It is an area that is unique to the human species. I suspect that there are no other organisms that engage in the kind of discussions such as we are having right now but it's a kind of thing that I will drop in favor of listening to any questions that you might have or any practical utility for the moment. So, go ahead.

CK: Well, I'm actually interested in what you have to say there but, with your philosophy and notion of what should we be doing in the future, what were your thoughts about that 20 years ago and have we accomplished any of it.

JK: You know that's a good question.

I have a feeling that we have not made a lot of progress, but I do think that the future interestingly looks as bright. It's just that we have not managed to focus our interests on the basic science part of this process. We have all been very fascinated by the practical utility in the treatment of specific disorders and certainly it is important because not only does it work but it also is helpful in providing a living at least a partial living—providing incomes for those who become professional biofeedback trainers. And that's not a small matter but I think that we are moving closer to using biofeedback as a self-reflective tool rather than a clinical device.

What I would have loved to see is more of us getting together and to help clarify our minds as to just what is this thing that we have developed in terms of how it relates to introspection, to the mapping of the total range of human experience ranging all the way from obvious sensory things like pains and the like, fatigue, all the way to abstract mathematical conceptions and how our verbal capacities have begun to play a role in tagging all of this stuff. This is still largely unexplored I think, or at least it seems that way to me.

Perhaps I'm being deliberately obtuse here, but I have the feeling that there is much to be learned especially because we have not had the capacity to monitor our own brain and body functions except in the last 50 years or so to any degree of sophistication as ongoing processes. Not just x-rays or whatever, but things that monitor the actual functions of the human brain and body I would like to take part in an effort by some folks like you and others to try to describe what it is that we think that the future of a highly sophisticated technology can assist, and in what kind of scientific study would it be? I could label it, something such as the "Scientific Study of Consciousness" or how consciousness is related to the mind and body or to the brain and body. I, at least, feel that that is still largely an unexplored area. Only a few starts, I would say, have been made on it. It's a statement that may be obvious, but I would love nothing more than an opportunity to meet with others to try to hack out more clearly where it is that we think that our technology can lead us. Thinking of these things on my own I can only get so far, yet I have the feeling that I would be very much stimulated by the opportunity to have an ongoing discussion, weekly or monthly, on a conference call or email, we could call it the "Science of Body and Mind." Let me just sort-of stop here because I think I begin to sound repetitious.

TC: Not really! But I would like to thank Cynthia for that question, which got us into such a nice track. Let me develop an open question that I'm going to kind-of develop: That in the history of science and in the history of mathematics there are countless examples of great discoveries that were predicted. Centuries and millennia before they were found. For example, Aristotle said everything is made out of atoms and it took 2000 years for us to discover that. Einstein said if you measure light going around the sun, you'll find that light bends and it took years for someone to measure bending of light and such. So, when these things get discovered they often refer back to the earlier prediction and say, for example, that you know—Hubble's theory was confirmed or Einstein's prediction was accurate. And now what I want to ask is: What is the "Kamiya Hypothesis?" What is the insight that we're going to look back to in 50 years and say the *Kamiya Hypothesis* led us to think this way?

JK: That's very good. I'm not sure I remember exactly what the hell my hypothesis was, but I can only give a sort of an autobiographical sort of a statement where my whole point or the sources of my preoccupations stem from, probably several factors, one of them a sociological fact—that I was a minority person and keenly aware of some of the prejudices, the other things that people operated in, which I had to work through. The other is a kind of introspective bent that I tended to have when I was in high school. I began very seriously to question what the meaning of life was. I got very depressed thinking about the fact that I didn't have the answer. And I remember getting on the school bus going to high school was about when this concern of mine started.

I'm beginning to really enjoy these phone calls because you know you have started the process so that I would love to continue until we are dead.

TC: Or in another dimension and I think that's where the *Kamiya Hypothesis* is going to send us.

JK: That's, for me, a kind of a mind-boggling thing to think about what we're talking about. Especially when you think about the fact that it is our evolution by natural selection that led to study about evolution.

TC: Yes.

JK: That has, I think, some very interesting implications. In fact, I thought it might be worthwhile, perhaps, at this moment to mention one or two that are thought of and I started jotting them down in my notebook because this stuff can easily evaporate if one doesn't write them down. So, let me get my notebook that I wrote these things down in.

TC: Oh! I'm sure it'll be fascinating Joe.

CK: Yeah, I can't wait for that.

JK: I'm completely, you know, mind-boggled by the implications of what we humans seem to be in or it could be in. Let me just simply tell you what I have written so far that partly reflects to the notions that I may have alluded to earlier. The notion is that evolution can lead to the study of evolution.

TC: Yes.

JK: And the classes cannot be fully predicted but some points seem safely stated:

1. The study of evolution led to the material base, that is to say that chemical mechanisms underlying species evolution.

2. Genetic modification can lead to changes in the distribution of intellectual power among the population.

3. Sexual selection of mates is likely to decelerate and/or accelerate the growth of the knowledge base of the human genetic. That is to say, that it is a self-feeding proposition, very much like the old natural evolution of the old days was.

4. The determinant changes in genetic chemistry should become a central issue for human history.

TC: Yes.

JK: And five: it is conceivable that genetic modification can focus on increasing intellectual capacity for more insight into the evolutionary process. Perhaps to improve mathematical insights—whatever. So, these are some of the things that I've just been speculating about and for whatever they're worth, I feel that this is an area that apparently. . . (I'm not at all widely read in this area and I feel ashamed about that because there's probably a hell of a lot more lying around in library books and scientific articles than I'm aware of.) But it's enough to get me started and I hope to do. So, I think that when we talk about the future of the human race—to call it, that we are talking about some very amazing things—not just the usual battles and wars and the elections and the like and the occasional specific mutants but we're also talking about things that we can ourselves control to some degree. If we want to and/or if we feel like we must.

I'm thinking of the science fiction guy who decides he's going to destroy the human race by modifying all of us back into monkeys. Or fight battles or do whatever things like that. But these are the kinds of speculative areas that had caught myself getting into and I probably should stop about this point because given the general flavor of it. The general point is evolution led to this study of evolution. Which led to the study of its material—that is to say chemical base, and it led to considerable power in the future studies of evolution and its control. And the social control of that control is probably going to become an issue and it is already. Perhaps some kind of evolutionary freaks are forbidden by law. But it certainly is conceivable that it will be heavily discouraged or encouraged as the genes may fall. So, let me just stop right there because that's about where my speculations are and that I don't know if these things are worthy of thinking about. But to me, I have a sneaking suspicion they will become issues in the future.

TC: I'm sure they will. Joe while you're talking, I'm also making notes. I'm going to do them one at a time though and let you talk rather than throwing them all at you. One of the first things that came to my mind is that if you define breeding as controlling the mating process so as to alter or regulate the setup—the distribution of a species, then what is the first organism or species that was bred by humans? And most people will say goats, you know, dogs.

But truly the first beings that were bred by humans are humans themselves. We took some role in our own self-selection for the reasons of physical appearance, stealth, strength, viciousness—you name it.

So, I'd like to ask you to speculate on what happened as humans began to control their own choices.

JK: Well that's the big issue. It is that I think it's worth it for all of us to speculate about and be concerned about because I could see some pretty risky policies that might be attempted by ill-considered plans. The whole notion of genetic modification is both a breathtakingly exciting potential as well as an ominous threat to the human situation.

It will take collective wisdom, which we hopefully will selectively continue to increase our capacities as we go along. But there we have it. It's one that is fun to speculate about, but which may not have much consequence at the present time. I should pause at this point. I think that what you just said is very important. I think what we need to do is to encourage further discussion of this kind of thing by many more people and people with much more background in very specific areas—particularly genetics, of which I am just a rank amateur. I suspect very a fruitful kind of a thing. There are other issues too, I suppose, that are worth thinking about. And let me not hog the conversation on just that one topic. So, what else can we talk about sir and ma'am?

CK: I think this is a really interesting discussion. But Tom, you said you had more notes, so why don't you continue?

TC: Okay great. Thank you. I have two more. One which has mystified me for a long, long time is: why do we have emotions? Why did nature conspire to make it so that I can feel good or bad? Often mostly bad because that's what gets me moving in the morning. My sense that something isn't done, that there's more work to be done. Why aren't we just programmed—like computers to do the right things? I once talked to Karl Pribram and my conclusion was because the Creator was bound and determined to make us unhappy. And he said that's exactly right.

CK: And why do you think that that's why these things exist? That our Creator wanted to make us unhappy?

TC: Because it gets us off our behinds.

JK: It aided in survival because of, let's say, disappointment. Another very obvious one is fear. It is very helpful to have the capacity to be afraid of the imminent threat of the simple, dangerous things like falling off cliffs, which we don't do because we have, through our earlier emotional developments learned very wisely to stay away from the edges of precipices. And in the control of personal relations—particularly of marriage relationships, I think it's very obvious that the emotions had to evolve to create some form of bonding and need to train or help others, particularly one's offspring. That does not seem to be a very emotional thing, but when you consider that sense of bonding, the parental bonding, that people have for their kids- that's an emotion that very clearly serves a survival function. And around this goes the happiness of successful bondings and fruitful ones. And, as well, goes fear of the forces that might threaten those kinds of relationships. For instance, jealousy about other people—about one's mate becoming potentially pulled off of the marriage situation from another party. The anger and hostility that creates obviously serves a very vital function in the preservation of marriage.

But it is does so when that anger is channeled with wisdom as a way to prevent further negative reactions in the partners. So, emotions evolved more so or have become the best example of evolutionary process in sustaining human life. That's my speculation right at the moment. So, I'm interested in what you have come to think about.

TC: Well that's certainly a novel insight for which I thank you. It, kind of, takes it to the full other extreme—that emotions are a pinnacle, rather than a pushing influence. But I still remain mystified. One could program a machine to take care of someone else. And people do that. So, the interesting thing about emotions to me is the contrast with the third point that I'm going to make and that is this use of words and language to try and communicate our internal thoughts and feelings. And I'll make a comment, Joe: you said though I'm sorry that you hadn't't read lots and lots of books about, you know, brain mind and evolution and such. I would posit that an enormous amount of that material is a verbal spiral that self-defines and self-serves and goes around and around in circles.

Words for all their power and all their strength are very destructive and ill-suited toward really expressing what's going on inside of us.

CK: And I agree with that, but I do want to say that words without emotion—like emails and texts and things like that, are much more disruptive than words with emotion.

TC: That's a good point.

JK: Well, certainly the emergence of the initial use of vocalization to communicate both about objects in the external world and events in the internal world such as angers and fears and love are quite vital to the development of the human species. And have been and really rremain so right now. The use of words to label these kinds of emotions and thoughts and feelings, etc.—the symbolic use of language has, of course, been an incredible means of development of the human species and probably underlies much of what we call intelligence—the intelligence of human beings. Because of the facility with which we can communicate, there are some things we otherwise would not be able to communicate, especially about feelings. So, I think the verbal development of the human race is certainly something to ponder. As far as I know there's nothing that matches the power of human speech capacity to be found anywhere in any other species.
JoK: I think that feelings allow us to share emotions with each other. I think that part of language is to allow us to communicate with one another and that not all communication is just emotional but it's a combination of those. Maybe something more subtle like qualia. There's a subtle quality that is an important part of the communication picture. We recognize those qualities and try to communicate that recognition to one another.

TC: Well that's interesting. That, kind of, is getting to why music works. That's another "ponderable:" why would music work. Why would we evolve to have music?

CK: We respond to drumming and rain—synchronous sounds like that.

TC: Sounds of nature

CK: Did these reactions became more sophisticated as our frontal lobes became more developed?

JoK: Probably. I mean we certainly—even in the cave painting environment it's been found that clusters of images were in places of extra resonance in those caves. Music definitely works. I think that it touches on all those aspects of being human somehow.

TC: Your comment about the caves and the resonance is fascinating because it elevates a whole new issue. What about all these influences and dimensions that we are totally unaware of? There's new evidence that static fields are, actually the electrical field of your heart, broadcasts to the person next to you.

JoK: I find that I get distracted with all that cultural noise and so on—my own noise or something. And I think it's very important to be able to pick up—tune in—to these things. Because they're there to be observed, shall we say registered. And I think that it's great that we can begin to take notice somehow.

CK: To articulate. We're taking notice. Our bodies are taking notice, but we are using language to articulate what that experience is.

JoK: Yes. And often the less articulated experience can be shared if there is a shared experience of that. It can be non-verbal and then it can rise to a more verbal level. It's a shared experience.

TC: Yes, but as the Buddhists point out—the word is really a pointer. And how do I know that my word is pointing to the same thing that it points to when you hear the same word? We could be pointing to two completely different things.

JoK: Absolutely.

CK: That message can follow just like perception of color.

TC: Absolutely. I could say green and you could say green. But our internal experience could be completely different.

JoK: Yeah. I think that that's where we look at convergence and begin to point to different greens we might mix up. I mean being an artist I would mix up a color that I think is the green. I mean, let's see if it's the same one you mix up. And they'll be different; they'll be very different. You know they will be different, but they will overlap too. They will have certain wavelengths that are in common. And if I were red-green colorblind they'll be more different. But it is a pointer. You're right. It's a hypothetical green, let's say.

TC: But how is that different from when two people say "Alpha" and they've both experienced alpha in a biofeedback situation. How is that different?

JoK: I don't think it is very different. But it depends on our similar neurophysiology, which helps nudge that toward a similarity of experience perhaps. But I think it's easier for people who have experience with alpha in a biofeedback situation to talk about it amongst themselves.

CK: I think their experience around alpha, their subjective experience, for example, how they know that they're in an "alpha state." There's no way that we would ever be able to quantify the subjective explanation of what their experience was: to be able to quantify it, or to say that two peoples' alpha is exactly the same. Just like with anything, one person's 10 could be another person's 3. We have no way of quantifying.

TC: Right.

JoK: Joe used to think we could.

CK: Go ahead, Joe—prove me wrong.

TC: Yeah! Tell us about it.

JK: I think that the issue of communication is crucial for the development of human traits. We would be nothing if we could not express our state of mind and feelings to each other in controlling our, and our children's, behaviors, and setting their goals and aspirations. And so, we are really on the threshold of improving our means of communication with each other. Right now, the feelings for each of you is left explained by a few words. I know I love you both. I'm excited by your presence and your interest in what I have to say. And I am pleased for the chance to talk about it. But you know, there's so much more to the total experience than just that.

Anyway, let's go from here. I would like to see what kind of agenda you would like to pursue at this point with regard to all this. By the way, I have apparently discovered for the first time something I should have known before that the two of you are planning to write a book about these matters and possibly even about me. Could I be clarified about what it is that you two have in mind? Or the end product of our endless conversations?

CK: We are recording all of our sessions and are planning a book. We are working to help you tell your story.

JK: Oh. OK. Well that's very good because that certainly has been my aspiration to write the story of my life. This would very much help me to do so and to use as a steppingstone for additional things. But I also know I'm in the position of thinking about what things instruct you. And we think about them in terms of what this book would be.

JoK: I think that one of your ideas, while not so much the *Kamiya Hypothesis*, it is the idea of using the convergence approach to discover hypotheses, and to not just test hypotheses, but to use the convergence approach to develop them.

JK: That is helpful. Thank you, Joanne. I think I sent to both of you that paper Stoyva and I wrote wrote on convergence for the *Psychological Review*. Did you get copies of it? I meant to do that. The basic idea is that it's the use of brain and body relationships to consciousness that will be richly rewarded because now we have a technology that would seem to be useful, and that technology is biofeedback and neurofeedback of course, with adding all of the advancements of electrophysiological and neurological science. The idea of convergence is, of course, basic to all sciences. That is to say, areas of knowledge are related to each other, and the more clearly we become how that relationship occurs or is, the better off we are as a sophisticated, knowledgeable as individuals, not quite as blindly going ahead in life as one might otherwise might, I guess. It's very easy to become over-personalized about this kind of stuff, but then by necessity, some of this stuff has evolved. Self-exploration tends to get wrapped up that way.

JoK: I think that using that approach, it gets back to first-person science, using the person's own observation in convergence with other indicators so that when they overlap you can develop hypotheses not just test them. It is all in the paper that you have.

Stoyva and Kamiya: *Psychological Review*, that paper is pretty old now. And now that I think of it, it's not that profound, it's simply an explicit statement of the logic of science of mind. I think it's the kind of thing that we all assume, I thought it was helpful with Johann, to spell out just exactly what was involved in the process of doing science of the mind.

CK: Wondering if you came up with a concise statement of what would be the Kamiya doctrine? What would be your motivations in terms of your career, and the efforts you put into science?

TC: Science moves by solving what we call "problems." For example, in physics, there is the "three body problem" that once you can solve it, you can go to the moon. There is a problem, which people think is a problem, called the "mind-body problem." So, I'd like to hear Joe's comments on the mind-body problem. Is it a problem, and can you predict in 50 or 100 years, what we are going to think of the mind-body problem?

CK: I suggest we ask this question in pieces. I'd first ask Joe, what is your perspective on the mind-body problem?

JK: My perspective is confused, but at the same time I have the gut feeling that it is the most important question of all times that is being posed. As a species we have come to realize that there are certain characteristics that have something to do with our relationships as a species—with one another, that is, that we could learn much about the world, and the world including us as evolved creatures, and where we are now compared with many, many years ago. Have we advanced beyond what Plato wrote in *The Republic*, or have we not? In some ways we have been surprisingly productive, I would think, but in other ways, I think we have some ways to go.

I feel as though perhaps I should answer some questions that have been put to me by email. One is by Aubrey Ewing, who requested some commentary, and I will look that over to see what can be useful. Do you think, actually, Tom and Cynthia, that the pursuit of this question is going to be fruitful or be useful for any reason at all? I'm not sure. (laughs)

CK: I think it is, yes, very much so.

JK: Well, OK, I will do what I can to let me say this. I am very much encouraged by the fact that you are at least interested in what this whole area is, and I will send a couple of things I have written in response to Ewing and to others, and also try to state what are some of the objectives that need to be met if we are to make any more progress in this area. And that might be the best thing that I could do at this point.

TC: Wonderful.

CK: Sounds great. How long ago was that?

JK: What was that question?

JoK: How long. Oh, a while. (laughter) Ewing sent you that question. It was, let's see.

JK: It was when my email was netcom.com.

CK: So, it was a while ago?

JoK: It was at least 8 years ago.

CK: OK. Well, if you still have access to that, that would be wonderful.

TC: Yes, it would.

JK: Yeah, but the date 2008, April 24, that is when Ewing wrote me.

JoK: That is almost 10 years.

JK: Yeah.

TC: Yes.

JK: OK.

TC: Well, thank you, Joe and Joanne for a very lively and spirited discussion. I look forward to really moving this forward so there is a Kamiya conjecture or a Kamiya hypothesis which I suspect will involve a relationship with ourselves and our relationship with others is some very profound way.

JoK: Yes, I think that some further thought about that is due. Thank you for the questions by the way. Your questions are like gold.

CK: How do you think that the current equipment we have would substantiate your findings from 30-40 years ago?

JK: Oh, I think it would go quite well. I think it would just be sufficient to start with a very simple demonstration that when people close their eyes there are quite different EEG patterns displayed especially the alpha rhythm and that when they open their eyes the alpha rhythm will come back but in much less frequent bursts, and however, as they then begin to imagine things in the mind's eye such as what does the letter "B" look like in reverse. With that kind of intense imagining, they will see a complete change in the absence of alpha. With substantial numbers of people that is—not everybody.

JoK: Cynthia, I think that you were asking about what kinds of activities might be introduced, I would think small groups of students, you know what I mean.

I don't think that we can necessarily hope to change the entire curriculum of a school district. That is not, sort of, how this starts.

Last time we talked, we talked about the mindfulness project that seemed to catch on. Things like that have been tried before, but this was uniquely successful, I think. For one thing, the culture may have had a chance to catch up with that idea a little bit. It wasn't quite so strange. But obviously there was a very skillful teacher and advocate that had worked with kids a lot and knew what to do to introduce this. And knew how to encourage participation of the students and of the parents and teachers and whatever.

CK: Absolutely, you definitely have to have the right person to foster and, you know, to shuttle through the right kind of encouragements and that kind of thing.

JoK: Yes.

CK: I was just thinking about, for example Tom's BrainAvatar, where you can actually look at the activity in your brain while you are doing neurofeedback using LORETA that looks very much like using MRI or fMRI.

JoK: Yes.

CK: It is very validating in terms of seeing those kinds of changes in real time while doing neurofeedback.

JoK: Absolutely.

CK: But I wonder if you guys feel that that is actually progress in the field or are we stepping away from really listening to ourselves in order to derive what state we are in?

JK: I think seeing that kind of thing in real-time is incredibly valuable.

JoK: Yes. I would say that, I would echo Joe's idea about the materials because in the instances, in the few long ago and far away instances that I have either participated in or known about, the teachers did that, I mean there were special materials that went along with the thing and that was good. To get back to Tom's Avatar, I would love to try that.

TC: We've got to get you connected.

CK: Yeah, we could do this.

JoK: I'd have a lot more to say about it if I tried it.

CK: Mm Hmm

TC: And so there seems to be some real rigidity that comes after a certain time and you will know we talked about upbringing and parenting and early childhood experiences. You've talked to Joe and know that we've got to get at the kids early on during these formative years. So, they develop a sense of awareness of their own mind and awareness of others and not a narrow-minded homophobic or xenophobic point of view. Once these get locked in, they seem to stay locked in, don't they?

JoK: Yes. Yes.

TC: It's almost pointless to argue with an adult about politics or religion.

JoK: Yeah that's true. But there I think that one thing that I have been negligent on myself is thanking the people who have done some good things. You know like I was thinking that we narrowly escaped the debacle on health care and John McCain went against his party. I am not his constituency and so on. But you know I can say thank you.

TC: Yeah, I agree with that.

JoK: People who stick their necks out or work particularly hard for us deserve thanks.

TC: Yep. They certainly do. These are very tough people who are working very hard, I mean he is not a young man either.

JoK: Oh, no.

TC: We have a very limited amount of time with people like John McCain who created his own character in the '60s and '70s. And I think we are increasingly finding cynicism and self-aggrandizement and self-interest becoming the watch word, at least for some people.

JoK: Yeah, so maybe we could, you know, reinforce the efforts of people with whom we agree with our thanks for their hard work.

C: Yeah.

JoK: Sometimes the hard work doesn't succeed.

TC: Yep.

JoK: If somebody loses an election then who bothers to say, "Thanks for the effort." You know? We'll get better next time. I just think that's something we could do.

TC: Yes. I agree.

JK: I have the following suggestion, Tom, for myself: it might be something worthwhile for you and others to do, likewise. Number 1: I'm going to increase my contact list of my friends with whom I have communicated only once every few years, if even then. And with some of them I have not communicated with for well over a decade, but for whom I have some feeling for them and I am sure they do for me. What I'd like to do is compile a list and ask for people to give their emails or their phone numbers or their mailing addresses. And get some of them to help me get their friends that I might know—so that I can begin to form a basis for a communication. And what I want to do once I get that—or even as I get—it is to start saying "Hey, what we need is a kind of a communication medium of what we ought to be doing for the advancement of our country and its welfare." And I would like to invite the other people to make responses to that so that we could actually begin to form a medium or media of communication that would help give us a little more coherence. Are you understanding what I'm saying so far?

TC: I think so, yes. And I we would be happy to help to foster this. We think it's a wonderful vision that you're putting out.

JK: Yeah, well you know like one of the things I need to do is to contact several of the people I know and some of them I have their older emails or their addresses or something. And I'm going to start asking each of them to send me the names of some of the other people that I will name that for whom I do not have contacts but whom I suspect they might have information so that I could increase my list.

Chapter 8
Some Colleagues

The sleep spindle is not limited to just certain classes of people, but it's universal.

CK: When did you meet Johann Stoyva?

JK: Johann Stoyva was a student at the University of Chicago, who happened to take a course that I was giving in Social Psychology. I started my career teaching social psychology. But at about the same time, within a year or two of teaching social psychology, however, I began to get interested in the use of the EEG in the study of sleep thanks to the work of such pioneers across the street, as Bill Dement, Nathanial Kleitman, and others. But the EEG itself then became of interest. And due to the fact that the University of Chicago has a very strong department on behavioristic approaches to things, I just naturally began to think in terms of the use EEG to explore, to train the discrimination and control of the brainwave as a method of exploring consciousness. And, Johann was with me at the time I was beginning to explore such things. He was one of the early subjects I ran, and he ran some of his own and got his PhD on the use of psychophysiology and with biofeedback. I have to confess; I've forgotten most of the details of what exactly we did – but he was my first student. There were other students who were around at the time. Some of them may have gone on to pursue careers in biofeedback, but I have not kept tabs on many of them. There were one or two. Sonia Ancoli is one. She came much later, but she is now at UC San Diego.

JoK: Oh, there were many others. But I'm thinking—didn't Johann actually come out here as a post-doc in the ITP as well.

JK: Yes, Johann came to join me as a post-doctoral fellow at the University of California and we had an interdisciplinary program in which I was a faculty member. Johann came to have me serve as his sponsor as a PhD in that program—as a post-doctoral trainee. Others came along in that training, including Karen Naifeh and Sonia Ancoli, who I already mentioned. Well, let me stop there and wait for next questions.

CK: So, if I understand you correctly, Johann was your very first student in the alpha state project?

JK: Maybe not the very first, but he was involved in doing that, yes. I have to confess; I've forgotten what he did finally do in my lab. We were very good friends. I have to say, maybe we are seeing the first signs of Alzheimer's?

CK: I would say, at your age, it's not Alzheimer's, it's just your age. It's what happens to our poor brains after we work them to death.

JK: Well, OK. Yes. I like to brag about the fact that I'm now 91 years old I and forget.

TC: That's wonderful.

CK: I'm going to change the subject. When Barry (Sterman) described the SMR spindle—you know there has been over the years question about whether it really is a unique spindle; that it might be a form of mu. Outside of our community SMR is not considered a viable spindle. It's thought of as just a sleep spindle or some other thing. I wonder if you can't recall when Barry was learning about SMR, what your reaction to that was.

JK: OK. I'd forgotten whether he told me when he came up to northern California and we talked about his work. I do know that he was excited about the fact that I had done the alpha feedback stuff and he wanted to get involved and to talk about that. But I know that he had already been quite active in EEG analysis of epilepsy and had then developed the feedback method to treat epilepsy that was successful. I believe, I think, talked with him shortly after his success with his first patient and it looked very promising indeed. He worked first with cats. He noted the behavioral, as well as neurophysiological, and concomitance of the 14 Hz spindle. So anyway, he certainly was a substantial contributor to the field from an early stage on. I admit to a certain satisfaction of ego for having been the person who'd told him about the method of feedback training.

I had not yet at that point, as far as I recall, written anything about it. As you well know I didn't write much of anything about this whole field. And when I did it was several years later. Anyway, that's what I recall about that.

CK: But when he was describing to you the SMR spindle. What did you think about that? Did you think that he discovered a new EEG morphology?

JK: Oh, yes! I quite agree with your question. Of course, it was a very important advance in normal functioning mapping itself because the sleep spindle is not limited to just certain classes of people, but it's universal. It is a reasonably good predictor of what the person will say about his state of mind whether he was still awake or falling asleep or beginning to dream or whatever or imagine things especially if more than just a few seconds of the first burst of the sleep spindles were allowed to lapse. Very often, at the very first occasion of the sleep spindle, or for that matter any other substantial change in the general state of arousal of the individual, often it is not a very good indicator. You have to wait for maybe a minute or so until the first seen wave form begins to occur more often and in a more prominent way in terms of the amplitude or duration of the burst, etc.

And when that happens within the one or two minutes that follows from when the first one occurs then you get quite sure that you're going to get a quite very different verbal report when the person is aroused and asked what his or her state of mind was.

JoK: That's different from the SMR.

JK. Yeah that's the sleep spindle. Not SMR. You're right.

JoK: I have one little personal observation to add to that. Which is: one time when we were at some conference and Barry hooked me up to his SMR feedback. And I had never done that particular thing before. So, I worked at it a little bit and then I seemed to catch on and he said, "Do you know what it was?" And I said, "Yes, it's what I got when I got absolutely still." And there was something qualitatively different. And it certainly wasn't falling asleep. It was just different.

TC: Yes. Barry has described SMR as reflecting the intention to remain still. And I'd like to ask you Joanne and Joe to think about the fact that if an EEG rhythm reflects something that was otherwise invisible—such as an intention, what the potential is now for the future of science if we can actually come up with new language and vocabulary to talk about things that were inside of us, but we never could communicate.

Like the bug in a box analogy that all of a sudden, maybe, I can describe my bug to you by giving how many legs it has, and how long it is, and what shape it is. And all of a sudden now we're able to go, "Oh my bug is different from yours." Or, "It sounds the same." I'm so fascinated what this means for human consciousness and I'd like you and Joe to tell me what your greatest vision might be for that.

JK: Oh, I think that's a very good, very apt statement of where we're at in the process of relating our conscious events to that part of the real world we call the brain—and body. That's very good. I think that it's that kind of mapping process that that represents and as we go on in this field, my hope is that we will be able to make our map more extensive and in different directions. I, in many ways, regret the fact that I don't have a lab anymore to start doing some of these things on my own. All I do around here is read the damned New York Times and San Francisco Chronicle, and argue with my wife.

JK: What did you say, Joanne?

JoK: I was saying hello to Tim.

JK: Tim who?

JoK: Tim Scully. He's now on the line.

JK: Oh! My God! Tim is on the line? I'm sorry, Tim. I want to think the process of aging has something to do with this. I will take most of the responsibility, damn it. How are you, Tim?

Tim Scully: Well, I'm good, thanks. I'm getting older too, though. It's happening to all of us.

CK: What I would like to do is, since we're recording this, I would really like for the two of you to talk about what it was like when you were working together. Was it in the 80s you guys connected and Tim was getting started putting together biofeedback equipment? And I just would like to hear you guys talk about that.

TS: I actually first met Joe in 1970 when I was starting Aquarius Electronics and I needed information about brainwaves and Joe was very helpful to someone who was very ignorant. He was very generous with his time.

CK: Tim said his first experience with you, Joe, was quite fruitful because he wanted to learn about the EEG, and he said that you were very generous with your expertise and your time with him.

JK: Joanne would like me to talk about the light sculpture that Tim and Jean Millay ran, and Joanne used at the San Francisco school. The kids were able to see and were completely fascinated by the light sculpture. It was a device that would show differences in brain wave activity.

JoK: It was the frequency of brain waves and there were 3 different colors.

TS: So, the light sculpture reading is from an instrument that I developed slightly later in the 1970s. The first instrument I built was with a single channel encephalophone. And it just allowed you to listen to EEG. And then I designed a gadget called the Brainwave Analyzer which has zero-crossing detection which put the EEG data into different frequency bins. The early version had the ability to detect beta, alpha, theta and delta. And, the gadget had little LEDs that would detect which brainwave frequency was dominant at the time – using zero-crossing detection to do this. Each half cycle of EEG was sorted into a bin determined by how long it lasted. And, there were banana jacks that provided a logic signal that mimicked what the little LED did, so that when alpha was turned on—or when beta was turned on, the beta logic signal was turned on.

And Jean asked me to build an optical isolator. Well, she didn't think of it that way. She asked me to build an interface that would allow her to control lightbulbs—powerful lightbulbs that plugged into the powerline and worked from those logic signals. So, I built an optical isolator for subject safely and a power switching kit that let her plug anything she wanted into it that could be turned on or off by each brain wave category. Then she inscribed patterns on sheets of tracing paper. We got her sheets of Plexiglas and she transferred the patterns into Plexiglass by drilling holes. So, she had these sheets of Plexiglass with the geometrical patterns that she'd drawn. We had a woodworker make a box that housed the Plexiglass in an array with lightbulbs mounted at the edge of each sheet that would be controlled by the brainwaves.

The earliest version of the light sculpture was single channel, so we were looking at only one channel of EEG—one scalp location. And, a later version was serialized with two sculptures and two channels of EEG. You could look at both images of one brain or you could look at two different people. Then you could compare what was going on with two sides of the brain, because the "stereo" light sculpture had patterns for each side.

CK: Well Tim, I'll bet that was really interesting for you.

TC: Yeah. Fascinating to hear, Tim about her (your?) early exploration. And I'm assuming all of this obviously used technology is the age of basic instruments and such. I guess I'm curious about the responses that you've gotten from the public—from academic and from the popular culture because you were one of the pioneers then. What were some of the more notable times that you showed us or had a response? Was it ever run on the media or anything like that?

Well, Jean Millay naturally evolved into being the person who got involved with the media. She's very gregarious and one of her geniuses is connecting people. So early on—back in 1970 when building the first encephalophone, she was at the Maimonides Sleep Lab with Stan Krippner, who was volunteering there. She met one of the editors of Life Magazine and turned him onto the AlphaPhone headset.

That resulted in a two-page article in Life magazine in the summer [August 21] of 1970 with a photo spread picturing my partner Frank Bakerich manufacturing headsets and a friend of mine, Gene Estribou, who was our distributor, with a room full of people hooked up to headsets who were doing brain wave training as a group.

That article resulted, of course, in many thousands of inquiries. We got buried in mail and that led to more media interest. Over the years, Jean did quite a bit of interfacing with the media. She was interested in parapsychology, so she lectured on the parapsychology circuit and she took alpha analyzers with her as she was doing it.

I was interested, initially at least, in the application of brainwave biofeedback training to learning meditative states of consciousness. I had been attracted by some of the research that Joe had published and some of the research that had been done with Zen monks and yoga masters showing that when they were meditating, they were producing massive amounts of alpha.

That lead to a lot of people trying alpha training with the hope that they would get into an interesting state of consciousness. It turned out that doing single channel EEG training didn't, as reliably as we hoped, correlate with a meditative state. There were a number of ways of producing a lot of alpha, and being in a meditative state was only one of them; that was only one of the possible states. But when Jean got me interested in making 2-channel EEG systems—she got involved with Russel Targ's research at Stanford Research Institute, in parapsychology.

TC: Tim, do you have any experiences with your systems where the individual was provided with some new insight or capacity that was recognizable that you could recount for us?

TS: Certainly. People did. It's hard to separate the placebo effects from the effect of the training they did, but some people reported, from doing alpha training, to be able to meditate or center themselves. As we got into more sophisticated instruments, the brainwave analyzer, people using the brainwave analyzer doing beta training, some found it to help with focus of attention.

When we got into brain wave synchronization training, interhemispheric training in one person—people who learned to produce phase-synchronous alpha described that as "dynamic focus and a meditative state—but a state that was easy to fall out of if you lost the balance." It was like the difference of flying a helicopter and flying an airplane. With an airplane, if you take your hands off the controls it'll keep flying straight and level. If you're flying a helicopter, it'll just fall off in one direction or another and go crazy. That's what the brainwave synchronization training felt like. You had to actively maintain an empty-focused consciousness to maintain a high-amplitude synchronized alpha. People reported those states as being interesting.

Jean was interested in training people for interpersonal synchronization. Some of those folks reported increased rapport when they were successfully trained for more synchronization. A feeling of closeness with each other.

TC: Fascinating! Well that's very important. This is what we want to know about.

TS: She wrote a dissertation about the study she did with that. She was trying to investigate how well people would do at tasks like telepathy when people were synchronized or when they weren't. Over time, I eventually got interested in additional physiological modalities. Galvanic skin response (GSR/BSR), skin temperature, electromyography.

I started building instruments for all of those things. During this time, Intel started producing microcomputer chips, so I got involved in building computerized physiological monitoring and biofeedback systems and that led me to look at more complex physiological patterns. And is, of course, a much better way of trying to narrow down the range of correlations you can have between physiology and consciousness. Any single physiological measure has multiple correlations with states of consciousness. If you look at enough physiological measures, you can narrow down the possible states of consciousness and still be in that physiological state. Of course, a lot of progress has been made since then with that idea.

TC: So, is there a particular reason you moved on, or you say you moved into other areas of biofeedback. Are you still involved in generally biofeedback or mental processes?

TS: Well, that's not the main focus of my activity at this time. As you probably know I was involved in making biofeedback equipment for a few years. And then in 1973 I was indicted for my past involvement in making LSD. Which is what I'd done from 1966 through 1970.

And so, I ended up being convicted and sent to the penitentiary. I got out on appeal bond. I had a few years in which to prepare for [a long time in] prison. I knew I was going to end up spending a long time in prison. I had a 20-year sentence. And that's the time when I designed the computerized physiological monitoring system. The first one I built was when I was out on appeal bond. After I lost my appeals I went [back] to prison. While I was on appeal bond, Jean Millay helped me get involved with the Humanistic Psychology Institute [Saybrook University's predecessor]. It was a new external degree program that had been formed and I was excited by it because there was the possibility that I could be a student while being in prison. And so, I was able to gather some experimental data for my dissertation project just before the Supreme Court denied my appeal.

So, while I was in prison—after I'd been there long enough to gain the trust of one of the staff members and get parts sent in so I could build a computer, I did the statistical work on my dissertation and I corresponded with Joe, who was very helpful to me as I went through writing drafts of my dissertation over the next couple or 3 years. Joe was very helpful in giving me advice and criticism. And I was fortunate enough to get my sentence reduced and get out to a halfway house in late 1979. And the way I got out is because Joe was able to offer me a temporary job as a research assistant in his lab at Langley Porter because a friend of mine had been able to give his lab a small grant to support hiring me. I couldn't have gotten out of the penitentiary that soon without having a job. And of course, that was an ideal job.

And I was living in a halfway house in the Tenderloin in San Francisco, commuting by bus to Langley Porter. And it was wonderful. Not only did I get to work in the lab, but Joe had a kitchen. The lab was in old house that had been converted into a laboratory and so it had a kitchen and I was able to actually cook my own meals which was a real treat after several years in a penitentiary.

And eventually the halfway house let me get overnight passes and I could just sleep in the attic of Joe's lab. Instead of sleeping in this really scuzzy hotel in the Tenderloin filled with people who were screaming at night. Not a very pleasant place to stay! You know basically the same folks who'd been in the penitentiary were there and they were behaving in the same way they had been.

So, when I finally got out of the halfway house and on parole in 1980, we'd run out of the money to support me to work at Joe's lab and I returned home to Albion and started up this new company to manufacture these computerized physiological monitoring systems. I sold one to Karen Naifeh, who was a researcher working in Joe's lab and who was doing a project that involved respiration and looking at CO_2 levels in the blood while looking at other physiology. And so, I got to add more physiological measures to the gadgets I was designing.

Joe was contacted by a woman from the Children's Television Workshop. They were the same people who produced the Sesame Street television program. They were planning to build an amusement park called Sesame Place and they were thinking about having biofeedback computer games there. And so, they contacted Joe to look for somebody who built those biofeedback computer games and Joe suggested me because I built a very crude biofeedback Pong-type game where I replaced one of the knobs of the Pong game with physiological data either from EMG or temperature or EEG so one of two pong paddles could be controlled by physiology. I started working with Joyce Hakansson, a lovely woman who had a position writing educational software.

Unfortunately, the Children's Television Workshop changed their mind and decided not to do biofeedback games. But by then I was sort of hooked on working with Joyce and I wrote other educational video games for her—which turned out to be a better way of earning a living. It was more effective way of making a living than making biofeedback instruments. I did the two things in parallel, but I was making a lot more money writing software than I was building instruments.

I was paying off a debt to the IRS, a fine of $10,000 for the conviction I had and tuition to HPI. So, the money was kind of a priority. In fact, I was reporting to a parole officer, who reviewed my finances every month and wanted to make sure that I was putting as much money as possible into paying those things off. So, he strongly encouraged me to do the work that paid the most. So, over the next 10 years I continued to design and build biofeedback instruments while I also was getting more and more involved in doing, just doing, things with computers. I started a company selling computers. I became an AutoCAD dealer and started installing AutoCAD systems, which in those days involved a lot of custom electronics work. And I wrote a lot of software for people.

At the same time, I was making biofeedback instruments but it, sort of, shrank into a smaller and smaller portion of my time because the other work was paying so much better. And at the same time the FDA was threatening to tightly control and regulate the manufacture of biofeedback instruments. The Biofeedback Research Society had morphed into a society that had turned from a research group into a group of biofeedback practitioners who were mostly interested in doing medical biofeedback on a fee for service basis ideally reimbursed by insurance. And, because of that they lobbied to make biofeedback a licensed activity regulated by the state. And they also like the idea of having the FDA regulate the manufacture of biofeedback instruments as medical instruments because they felt that it would validate their practice with insurance companies and make it easier for them to get money from Medicare, or from major insurance companies.

So, my interest diverged from the mainstream of the biofeedback community because I was much more interested in what healthy people could do with biofeedback and less interested in the medical stuff. A large fraction of the instruments that I was building were custom designed. I usually wrote custom software or built custom hardware for various people and that sort of ad hoc instrument design is definitely frowned on by the FDA. They want you to design an instrument, get it software and hardware approved and then don't change it without a very expensive approval process.

So, I don't know if FDA actually ended up regulating biofeedback instruments that way, but the threat of it was one of the things that pushed me towards just writing software.

TC: Got it. I understand. Yeah, there remains significant barriers.

TS: Eventually Autodesk hired me as a consultant, and I ended up working 60 or 70 hours a week for them for quite a few years. They paid extremely well.

It was a lot of fun working with people who were smarter than I was and learning new stuff. It wasn't psychophysiology; I had fantasies that I would go back to doing psychophysiology when I retired from Autodesk. But then, during those years while I was working for them, a young filmmaker contacted me and he'd written a screenplay about the adventures I had with Owsley and the LSD underground. The main thing that came of that was that I introduced him to Owsley who was living in Australia by then and we ended up talking with Phil DeGuerre, who was a more mature film producer about the possibility of a film project about the history of underground LSD and that lead to several months of intense email conversations between Bear [Owsley] and my friend Don Douglas who was involved along with Melissa [in the labs we worked in], exchanging stories about what we've done. And during that time, I got interested in the idea of trying to gather and preserve the history of underground LSD making.

The film project never really materialized. We were unable to agree on a business model, which is probably just as well. However, I got hooked on this project of gathering history of the LSD manufacturing underground. I was interested in what happened to the people I've been involved with and with trying to make peace with my own conflicted feelings about what I'd done. So, one way or another, when I retired from Autodesk that became my major spare-time activity. And that's what I'm still working on now. I'm working on writing a memoir right now.

TC: Wonderful. Well, Tim—we're amazed to be able to be talking to you at this time. You were involved in so much world-shaping activity. In so many ways!

TS: Well for me to get involved in making biofeedback feedback instruments which was a marvelous way to kick the habit of making LSD, which was very intoxicating. We had the notion that we were trying to save the world. It was really hard to come down from that to a mundane job. But I was able to, for a few years at least, think that maybe we could turn the world on to alpha waves instead of LSD.

TC: Well I think that it's turning out that you were right on both counts. There's an enormous emerging evidence of the values of psychedelics in treating PTSD and other serious mental disorders. And again, biofeedback is holding its own and alpha and, specially, alpha theta training. Those two interventions are probably superior to anything else out there—whether it's cognitive behavior or medications or running around in the woods screaming. Somehow you really were on to very important

Chapter 9

Funding and Research

I think it's fine to go on one's own for a while but that doesn't amount to anything until it can impact others. And so as soon as we can begin to impact others, I think the better off we're going to be.

CK: If I were a foundation that had unlimited funds to grant you, what would your research look like? What would be the methodology?

JK: Oh—the research methodology, essentially the discrimination training and also training in verbal reporting of events. I think people need to be a little bit sharper in terms of the words. I would try to propose getting individuals to be a little bit more diversified and more differentiated, I should say. And the words that you use to characterize their internal state, that would be a part of the training program. Well, Joanne is an avid listener here and has a question:

JoK: Well, I want to say that we did something—Joe and Jim Johnston did something back in the day. It was different because we had the old PDP15 (which is not the greatest instrument for doing real-time brainwave studies). But one of the things that they did was to have a button that people would push while doing the feedback studies. It's like the time machine of the Apple back-up, you know what I mean? It would mark that section that had come just right before, and it could then be associated with internal state. The person would mark their own record, indicating that was the time in which whatever they were feeling or perceiving or thinking would coincide then with the EEG and maybe the eye movements or the brain waves or breathing things or something like that. It would mark those segments, but we were very limited in what we could do with that. While the idea was to have the person, who was running as a subject, be investigator and use that device to—as close to real time as possible—mark the significant episodes.

JK: That's very nice. I'm very grateful that you spoke up because I had forgotten that part. I think that's a very good strategy to use. And I would certainly research that today with the modern equipment. However, to answer Cindy's question:

JoK: We did it and it would work, but you know, we were limited in what we did.

JK: Yeah. It's approaching in the matter of a mind-brain relationship to them in a different way to help to provide certain supplemental and supportive information converging on a better concept than we currently have. So that would be very good. Oh, by the way, I have not mentioned converging. I wrote a paper in 1968, I think it was, on how the convergence of, concepts and observations upon hypothetical constructs was a very important process in science and that we needed to learn to look at ways in which any particular observation or idea needed supportive evidence from different sources. For example, in a very limited way, the fact that the eyes moved in a very specific way during stage one sleep indicated a greater probability that the person would report dreaming then if the eyes didn't move, even though there was the EEG pattern. And so, this would be the indication that it worked.

It is all police work. In all detection work, of course, one should seek clues of different kinds that will help converge upon the truth. And that's essentially what one does with EEG studies.

Actually, when you think about it, we take a piece of information, a data series of the EEG being trained in a particular way, and we then become very curious about a possibility that the same kind of ideas surrounding our discovery, are stimulated by a different kind of operation and a different kind of scientific study.

So, to answer your questions about what I would include, it would certainly include a discussion of the importance of convergence. And I would be sure to site my reference from 1968 about EEG and eye movement as converging indicators that are recording sleep. Anyway, I would, by the way, suppose that this be done, perhaps under some kind of a committee body that would form a kind-of a coordinated attempt by several different laboratories observing the relationship, let's say, of the EEG to emotions and consciousness. Then the reviewing bodies would review the grant proposals and talk to each other. And seek to fund and support those particular proposals that would tend to supplement each other in a growing body of converging evidence. I think that's not too much for a single paper that proposes a strategy of research in this field. It could describe what ought to be done in the future in terms of administration of research at the public level.

Uh, let's face it, the government—through NIH has played an enormous role in the development of health sciences and to some degree psychology as well.

It was probably unique in the world in terms of how fruitful that program is. I think there will be those of us who are wanting to do research in these areas. And we should have a supportive governmental activity that would encourage this type of research. I think that one single person can make some progress, yes. But hey, two or three different parties, two or three different laboratories, studying the particular issue and could begin to see some breakthroughs developing out of the cooperative activity of the groups. And, in some cases, yes, even competitive activities. Because we are ego-driven animals and we sometimes like to push hard for our own a pet projects and sometimes even seek to defeat the others. But in doing so in the end, if the arbiter is the evidence as opposed to just playing argumentation, then there is a positive gain. But from human beings being ego-driven as they are, if we can harness some of the ego activity collectively—as a productive unit, this calls for a much more enlightened, administrative activity. And so, the list goes beyond what you are currently raising. I think I should stop now because I've maybe gone too far afield.

TC: What, for example, was the funding situation and what was the climate like and how was your experience to build this research project and to get others including NIH or NSF interested.

JK: OK. Yes. Well the funding, in my experience, it was remarkably good. I did not get turned down for research grants. I might have gotten cut down in quantity of dollars from the grants. NIH—more specifically NIMH, was the group that seemed to be quite responsive to grant requests. And that's what I was able to go on.

Also, I had a career grant from NIH and NIMH. It was for career people giving five-year salary-paid grants with money going to the institutions to pay the salaries of the researcher. I think it was something like "Career Development Awards," something like that. I was able to get one of those. They lasted for five years. And that was independent of—in addition to—the research funding of the actual research operation. So, the funding was quite favorable for me—at least at the beginning.

But it began to dwindle down. It was also due to the fact that I, myself, was beginning to dwindle in terms of ambitions I suppose. I had, I have, a problem of writing and much of the research that I do took a long time for me to get it written and sent out for publication. And I think because that was difficult it tended to cause me to do idea development in research without publishing it. And that's about where, sort of, my career ended up, I guess. I would like to at least revivify – at least, the theoretical part of it. And that's where things stand now.

JoK: Joe also got a number of grants, some from foundations after the NIMH climate changed because the political situations changed, as we all know. And for a while his work in the EEG of performance was funded by ARPA (then, now DARPA).

JK: That stands for Advanced Research Projects Agency.

JoK: They were the ones who bought Joe the PDP15, for instance, and you know that that was useful and helpful. And then there were some others. There was the Babcock Foundation, other foundations, and then small grants. When I was working with Joe at the lab Charles Furst and I got a small grant to do something with EEGs – a very, very specific project on eidetic imagery. There were lots of smaller things like that that were sort of useful in supporting the research. But after a while NIMH funding got harder to get.

Partly, also, they would do things like say, "Approved but not funded," because they didn't have the money. It did matter. You know that's eventually why Joe started doing that stuff with NASA—because that was a way to pay the bills.

TC: Well, that's interesting. I'm not sure we are very aware of what was done with ARPA or NASA. Are there research reports that are not generally published?

JoK: Yeah, I think so. What Joe did with ARPA was a continuation of the basic research. Not only on EEG alpha, but also on the rest of the EEG spectrum. Some development of slow wave potential monitoring—things like that. And those were interesting. That's not quite what they wanted. They wanted to know how alpha would enhance performance.

JK: The person who was handling the research grants for psychologists was a guy named George Lawrence.

JoK: And before that it was Verne Johnson—from San Diego. But Verne Johnson was not with ARPA.

JoK: No, he was with San Diego Foundations. But it was funneled through his organization.

JK: That's right. ARPA was set up as a federal granting agency. And it was apparently administratively-free of NIMH.

TC: They built the first Internet. I mean they created TCP IP, which was originally DARPANET.

JoK: Yes. OK. DARPA grew out of ARPA.

TC: Absolutely. Yeah, we were part of that back at Bell Labs in the 80s. It's fascinating Joe. We'd love to know: tell us more about the work that was done for ARPA—what you found and was it possible that there is anything of value that we would love to know about.

JK: Well, let me see. I blended my work with the ARPA pretty much with the work that I did with NIMH. So, it's hard for me to say exactly what ARPA did for me. They became an auxiliary source of funding.

TC: So, in general we're interested in how the research progressed while all this work was funded.

JoK: A lot of the work was done with EEG biofeedback and in particular, Joe was interested in pinning down more about EEG alpha—how that was best described and so on. He did a lot of work on training and the best ways is to train people.

JK: I should also add that ARPA tried and succeeded, I think reasonably well, to create a research group of its funded people. We had annual meetings, paid for and sponsored by ARPA, discussing the various kinds of mostly biofeedback-centered studies. Gary Schwartz was also one of the recipients of the ARPA thing. If he's around still, he might provide you with some memories.

JK: So, I discovered that people could learn to discriminate and control alpha rhythms. The important part that was discovered by me—and I'm sure everyone knows by now, was that having learned to discern the difference, one could also learn to enter into the state of alpha. That is to say, "to control alpha." Even to diminish alpha—which led to the disappearance of alpha. And everyone got all excited about the control factor. To me, that's the most important thing in life—to control things. For me, what's equally important was that we could discover our states of mind—at least partially, and because they're correlated, at least sometimes with a physiological process that we can tag.

The future is so bright of course in the whole area of how to improve upon the various subjective states that are associated with different kinds of technologically definable events, in EEG especially, as well as other bodily processes.

The human social nature is capable of being explored as simple as using turn signals and brake lights while driving. What we need is more expression of gratitude to others in communicating internal states. We have all kinds of turn signals and brake lights in everyday life, it's really worth the cost of living to learn the other world of other people and ourselves. I am optimistic that the technology of the measurement of concomitants of consciousness can go a long way in conveying what our existence is about.

Those who know neurofeedback will help using these instruments, this technology, in education to help learning. As purveyors of this instrumentation, Tom, you are certainly part of the team in this expansion.

TC: Your key point of a team is important. For example, when we explore the sea or space, we have this idea of a team. And the team is trained, and the team has special equipment. The team has expectations and the team has goals. What would a team of Mind Explorers be like? What would be the training? What would be the equipment? The expectations? The closest thing to this today might almost be like a Buddhist monastery—particularly Tibetan.

JK: We would need the Buddhist approach to things. OK. Well, I think some of it may be unpredictable at the moment but very clearly all of us should have the optimum capacities of computers, and information processing. That goes without saying. And the equivalent of supercomputers should be available to the team. Simply because of the mass of information in supercomputers.

Nature has built-in codes that we have just begun to understand. We just have to keep working at this over time. We have to consider this a very long- term process that no one of us is going to be able to crack open the key to understanding human cognition and human emotion in natural terms.

We need to start training and educating children in this process. We should not discourage children's use of technology. Their fresher insights would become more and more available. How do we do that? I'm not totally sure.

We should not discourage the interest many children have in the use of technology. And I think it would be important to encourage those who show talent along those lines. Giving them a lot of social recognition and rewards and so on so that other kids will aspire to reach new heights. I think it's a matter of developing a reward system that is based on some reasonable standards that can be developed perhaps by the adult world that would help develop the process.

You have to think of this as probably a generation or two project that is going to have to be carefully managed by discussion such as the one we're having right now. Just exactly what would we do to encourage and develop talent in kids—and in ourselves too. I think of this as, sort of, a "cracking the code" process. It happens to be in the news right now in terms of accusations by our president about cracking code and snooping into CIA-type materials.

TC: It's inspiring to think of that. That sounds a little bit like support of the arts. And the support of what would be considered abstract science. And what would I want to know more about is how we can convey the importance and value of this? And I'll make an example that when the space program was in its early years, people first of all talked about, of course, the political and even military benefits of having space technology. But also, they talked about the secondary benefits with computer microchips and materials science and medical science. So that that program had benefits that accrued to the world from that exploration. And one thing I'm interested in is what will be the benefits in the greatest sense of having people conduct the scientific exploration of the mind. You've talked about social benefits. I'm now thinking about mental health benefits. Not just to treat disorders but, for example, to be more healthy in the way a mountaineer or a hiker is more healthy or a swimmer is more healthy. Would not a mind explorer be more healthy? Might he'll have better mental health than someone who is not engaged in mind exploration?

JoK: Thinking about this, one of the benefits and also one of the approaches is often in very small informal groups—or small research labs or small companies, small classes in schools. I've had the experience of working with kids and adults too, just having a technologically-assisted group exploration of something and it can be a variety of goals. But I think that my experience tells me that a few folks involved in a learning experience is helpful. It sparks insights and ideas grow. And then the technology grows, and the applications grow with a small group of folks working together. Each person doesn't need a whole set of equipment, people can share equipment and share insights.

TC: What would these participants be like? What will be their background? What will be their motivation? For example, using the space program, they were all test pilots or doctors or engineers. What they shared was this sense of the future, I believe.

JK: Maybe we ourselves could get a small group together and invite them. Get somebody to be the leader and just start inviting commentary and ideas from a variety of folks. We have some, I think, some pretty bright people in our midst and with lots of very interesting background experience working with people. And I think it will also be helpful to us to learn how to learn in this area. Certainly, for me it will be important to be able to learn with others.

I think it's fine to go on one's own for a while but that doesn't amount to anything until it can impact others. And so as soon as we can begin to impact others, I think the better off we're going to be.

TC: There are some possibilities. We need to be more precise of what the vision is. We are starting to push into social and political issues and what motivates groups to devote themselves to certain things. I see little things about Plato's Republic and how people react so badly to being shown the illusory sides and they actually can tend to rebel and oppose that type of thinking.

We need a slogan or mandate for people to realize this is important. One idea: schools that integrate mindfulness or meditation and even recess. Basically, many schools have taken away recess—believe it or not.

JoK: I imagine the kids get extremely hyperactive.

TC: So, we need the articulation of the direct value and benefit and what I would go so far as to say, 'urgency' of what you propose, which is getting this into schools, getting groups, getting labs. It's not hard to get kids interested in their cell phones and their texting. It's not hard to get them to play paintball and laser tag. What will it continue to take for self-exploration and mindfulness to be supported and become mainstream and be respected and actively supported and sought?

CK: Interventions that include exercise and nutrition and sleep. Mindfulness may be tolerated. A "mind explorer" needs to be active in order for mindfulness to work. And teachers need patience and devotion to the learning process. Kids need this instead of quick fixes such as meds or detention.

TC: Where does this leave us? I'm interested in any ideas you have about these. It's a systemic benefit of lifestyle. Mindfulness, mental fitness, and meditation are not just standalone goals. So how do we rebuild our own minds?

CK: We exercise, control our diet, sleep, and practice mindfulness.

TC: You know this gets me thinking; I heard Ram Das speak decades ago. And he said. "Pretend that on the side of your head is a channel selector and you've been looking at the same channel all your life but now you know how to turn that channel selector on the side of your head so you can see the world through these different channels." And he kind of challenged us to say what is it like if you change the channel of your vision and of your thinking? So, I'd like to see if anyone has any thoughts along that kind of a line.

CK: So, it's sort of like remontaging.

TC: Yes—it's a lot like remontaging. It's a lot like turning the filters off.

CK: Yeah. It's recreation. The word is re-create. You need to put out and take in. We end up putting out, putting out, putting out and we don't take enough in. And so, we need to stop. You know that old "stop and smell the roses" kind of thing. We need to stop and refresh and re-create.

JK: When Joanne has brought our biofeedback devices to elementary or high school children, they are very interested. They learn enormously. It's an extraordinary thing to children when they see a galvanic skin response go off when they are embarrassed. The child learns enormously when witnessing that kind of working in the body.

We need similar devices in a large group of classroom demonstrations so they can see the same biologic response being monitored. This should be tried and written about. It would be a way to combine this with Mindfulness. We could have classroom demonstrations by teachers in the public school system.

TC: We wrote a grant a number of years ago that proposed to put EEG monitors on a classroom of school children and it was not funded. It was very badly received by the granting agency. One of the reviewers said, "This is Orwellian." I believe it's like it is a taboo. There is actually a book called *Taboo* that is against finding out who you are. People fear going inward for some reason. We do seem to have a taboo against self-awareness. Any thoughts?

CK: I agree with that 100%. Let me answer the first question and that is that in all the years that my two girls were growing up pretty much every year they had Parents' Employment Day, when you go and show what you did for a living and do a demonstration. I would say pretty much every year from early education all through high school, I would say once a year if not every other year I did a demonstration on biofeedback. But you know I did biofeedback presentations and they're really fun. I'm sure Joanne can speak to this too. They're different, obviously, for a 3rd-grader than they are for a high-schooler.

You always get those one or two students that can really relate to the physiological experience. The first-person experience, if you will. And you change those kids—they learn something. But for the most part, as the kids get older, they lose interest in being internal. They grow away from an introspective perspective. It becomes more complicated to get their attention.

JoK: Yes. I would be interested in hearing more about what your experience was because I think there's some very practical aspects to this that we should pay attention to. The younger they are, in a sense, the better, in terms of the straight out just hooking up and seeing what's going on in the internal state. A friend of mine that was a teacher in a continuation high school did a voluntary classroom activity with those students coming before school at 8:00 in the morning. They loved it. They showed up. And she had an interesting approach with them. But as you say, that isn't always the case and she was really was devoted to it. She knew how to explain this to the kids without threatening or embarrassing them. The school didn't care what she did. These were the delinquent kids that showed up. So, I agree that age is a factor.

CK: Yes, and even college students should be involved, we want to reach out and affect people as early as we can and in our own special way. And timing is everything. People need to be ready to do the work and we need to be there at the right time.

JK: The actual technological aspect of this. It's important for students to see that their response to "fuck you" is universal at the grade school level.

Therefore, if you could provide the demonstration in a group setting, so that the child not only sees or hears his own response, but that similar responses are a universal aspect to human experience that is based biologically as well as socially. And as we discuss this, I wonder if it might be fun to have a group of us write down the basic components of a demonstration for school children at all age levels? What kinds of physiologic measures would be useful? Certainly, the GSR—everyone gets excited by that modality. It's easy to implement. You can show it as potential changes or resistance changes. It's been fairly universal and used since the birth of psychophysiology, years and years ago. That's one idea I would be very happy to contribute to.

And, as we talk, it would be fun to propose different demonstrations to be taught by teachers. We could write how to use it for demonstration to different age groups.

TC: I think that's exciting. I see things like bias and prejudice, being impacted in young kinds—in what we call theory of mind could be demonstrated. Being able to understand that someone has a mind that has something to do with yours. Fascinating ideas.

CK: Yes. The frustrating thing is how to practicalize them.

TC: That's a great concept—how to concretize this in education, especially with children.

JoK: We all have had some experience in these things. We could pool our experiences together. I've tried it when it was much too soon—at least for some people. But as Cynthia said – there's always one or two that really got it.

CK: And it's so satisfying to help those one or two people—really, to change their lives.

JoK: Maybe that's all we can hope. Maybe we can't, you know, sweep everybody into the basket at the same time (or jump in ourselves. . .). It's inspiring to think about this again.

The future benefit of the technology will be in what I call self-exploration and which I think Tom has sometimes called "First Person Science." The neurofeedback device makes it possible for us to interact with our brains in a manner that had not been available before in history. And what that portends for the development of the introspective side of human life is a bit hard to predict but I believe that it would be tremendously helpful in many ways just for the development of pure knowledge about human function but also of course applications will be found in many areas.

For instance, the whole process of the physiology of recovery from infections to the physiologic and psychological processes in the brain during trauma recovery or the kinds of things that are involved in the development of the brain in childhood and ways in which the educational policies can be tailored so as to not stifle the growing curiosity and interest to children—but encourages it.

And, in particular, as I see the future of this field very closely, potentially at least, high in the development of social processing for people like you and Tom right now. While talking, we could be connected to our own devices and we would be able to see the result of each of our instruments so that now we are having a real good -not only a "heart to heart," talk but a "brain to brain" talk that goes along with our, otherwise normal, conversation.

It's a little bit hard perhaps to foresee all the ramifications of what's going to happen. But if we could form small communities—temporary ones, with our mates or with friends locally. We hook ourselves up and observe each other as well as our selves physiologically at the same time. That is something that I think most definitely should be explored.

JK: We may be pursuing something that's out of reality, but I'll tell you one of the things I have learned about myself is that, if anything, I am a social creature. That I am born to be part of a social system and that when I try to overcome that by declaring that I am my own master and to hell with the rest of the world things fall apart. One he gets depressed, and one gets out of sync with one's mate, with one's children, with one's parents. The central part of being human is being human.

And I think we can help illuminate that process in a way or at least throw additional light on it that would be helpful for all of us. This is kind of futuristic talk, but I don't see any reason whatsoever that we can't make some trials with it and people, like Tom especially, who is involved in the development of instrumentation would be instrumental in the development of such devices. I would think of nothing else but getting the entire public-school system involved in teaching children the simple facts of what their brains and bodies are like as they experience and as they interact with people.

And this is just a part of the general education of the human being, of which I may sound a little futuristic. Let me just hang in there for a while and finish my thinking. This could really be a very important step forward in the development of our social interaction processes with each other. So, I stop right there.

CK: So then in answer to my question you're saying that with the advent of the more modern equipment one can be a bit more lazy in terms of self-introspection.

JK: Well yes. So, OK. Yet, I don't know if that's bad. I would think that this natural process of being curious about the world and about us would propel us forward in the use of these devices without any particular pathological processes to be curing but simply for one's self education, which I suspect will be a very important process of learning how to overcome the various kinds of problems that we experience as we grow up and with our interaction with our peers and the public school system, and the legal system. We would be much more in contact with ourselves and with the social system because we would now be able to tap into, with some of the independent monitoring devices, that which is happening in our bodies and brains that had not been possible before.

Chapter 10
Philosophical Musings

Because, let's face it, our thoughts are made possible by structures in the real world known as brains and bodies – that we know. And we have begun to catch glimpses of what's happening in the brain and body as we think, as we image, as we get angry, as we get afraid.

Being retired for ten years, Joe deeply looked forward to the weekly meetings. During our interviews, he wanted so much to know how Tom and I were doing personally and what we were doing professionally. To him, these interviews were more about group introspection and discussions about how to use biofeedback outside the clinical arena. He and Joanne always hoped to have biofeedback in the school setting, and this was often discussed. Joe mused, "[M]aybe I'm lost in the clouds, the human capacity for introspection is greatly assisted by the technology of measuring the brain. For the future, one application might be public schools—teaching students how to solve problems as they think about their lives. It need not be restricted to headaches and other clinical applications, but also for self-exploration and self-discovery, arts and science. We are only at the threshold of using this technology."

Joe went on to say, "I think everybody ought to own an EEG biofeedback device. For a few hundred bucks, everyone could have a sophisticated piece of equipment. The reveries and thoughts, the kind of resentments one may have, may be detected by EEG technology."

TC: Joe, I'd like you to use your imagination as much as possible and talk about the possibilities for exploring of, what I will call, "inner space." And I know so many people are interested in outer space and I read an article that was so interesting. It said that if we want to contact civilizations from other worlds, we ought not to look outside into the outer space, but we need to go inward because advanced civilizations will have explored inner space—the world of consciousness and pure awareness.

JK: The scientist in me, and the reasonable person in me would say, "That's hogwash."

JoK: Come on, now, Joe!

TC: So, what are the prospects then for humanity to explore inner space?

JK: OK, let's speculate about how that might come about. We have, of course, to recognize the fact of human evolution, and that it is possible, I suppose, that the earth was populated by people who, at one time, had developed far more psychologically in terms of internal perceptively etc. and knowledge and general wisdom, if you might call it that. Then maybe they regressed or were that way when they came here. But we managed to get some of those genes, and they survived and resulted in the human being with his capacity for introspection for developing his internal world. Or at least to explore and to come up with ideas about what constitutes the truth, and beauty, and all things like that. And to create things of their own—the worldly process of the things that clearly separate the human species from the closest cousins in the link in the evolutionary scheme.

That difference is quite conspicuous especially when it comes to the internal world exploration. This is an assumption because it may well be that the chimps sitting in their wild home in Africa or in zoos are actually pondering some pretty high-level stuff that we haven't got the faintest idea about. (That would be speculative.) It's reasonable to expect that is not the case because we assume that wisdom translates into language and is communicated and is not wisdom otherwise. So, on that ground I think perhaps we might reject the notion that other creatures and other peoples in our world do not communicate. Or they do in a language that is not in any of the ways of verbal communication that humans use. If such people existed, we would know it. And, I would think, they have some intuitive sense about our origins being somewhat different but at the present time as far as I can guess. . . Oh, I have managed to lose my train of thought because this is an area that is foggy for me. But let me try to pause right now and then restart what I think about this I am trying to say.

TC: This is an area where most minds never go. So, you get to be forgiven.

JK: I think that it is possible that people in the past thought like this and that they are those who achieved great wisdom. When we think about Plato, for example, we think, "Hey, you know this guy existed—I don't know—must be at least, certainly before Christ and maybe 1,000 years before, I don't know." That could be pinned down because I think scholars know exactly when he existed. But everybody recognizes that here was a man of great wisdom—but note, he was of great wisdom because he spoke—because he communicated.

Wisdom seems to consist of knowledge that is recognized by others through the processes of communication. And wisdom is, in a sense, therefor a social product. It is, at the very least, always dependent upon single individuals reflecting about the nature of things. But then talking about it to others who listen and can be stimulated by it and then talk to others and to the first person and a body of knowledge gets developed as a result of the combination of the introspective activities of different people communicating with each other.

And, in some cases, people writing things down for themselves and engaging in a kind of a dialogue with themselves that way. But, in any case, the place of language is always necessary to recognize and that is a kind of an interesting thing because the language itself is kind of a thing that seems somehow to be adapted.

Anyway, that's one point of wisdom and this internal awareness, this notion that I think you're trying to get me to talk about which is the higher consciousness—consciousness itself, etc. These are the terms that we are concerned about, I think. And I actually think that we're in a position now, as humans, we are slightly better to think about the nature of consciousness because we have become aware of our ties as a species biologically. And I think it's a very important step because it ties us with very concrete pathways to the connections that we have with the rest of the world, including other creatures. I think that in the past it was not really thought about very clearly at all. Maybe even guys like Plato himself really didn't know a hell of a lot about his brain structure or his evolution or his relationship to other species and how he came to be. But still without all that he appears to have established an incredibly smart conception of what we call "the truth" in his book *The Republic of Plato*.

TC: I believe language is a singularly poor way to capture meaning and I'll show the example of when we put a word on some item. Let's say the word, "chair." When I identify something as the word chair, I ignore its individuality and I collapse all chairs into one thing. And to me that is a destructive type of step to take because it denies the primacy of experiencing a chair. So, what you described to me, Joe, is intellectual history "before Joe Kamiya" came on the scene and that you describe the verbal and written intellectual tradition as pre-Joe Kamiya intellectual tradition. We want to get beyond words and go straight to the experience.

JK: How will I know your experience?

TC: Well let's pursue that. But I want to throw out one more comment, if I may. If you read Alan Watts, and if you read D.T. Suzuki, the traditions of Zen and even Japanese Zen, one of my favorite sayings which is actually captured in four Chinese characters basically says, "the Zen which can be spoken is not the true Zen."

So, I ask you to think about the intellectual tradition that cannot be spoken or written in language. And how do we create a framework for studying a non- language-bound study of experience and consciousness?

可以說的禪不是真正的禪
Kěyǐ shuō de chán bùshì zhēnzhèng de chán

JK: OK. You can do so through this thing called art through painting, through music, through poetry, through whatever. Poetry is a good one because it uses words, but it does so in an artistic way and it does not consist of sentences, but it carries some kind of music-like flow—some kind of meaning to the listener.

So, what I think is that, well let's see: Let me stop tossing for a moment—to sort—of think. I tend to just kind of blab off the first thing that comes to mind, and it sometimes catches me with its inadequacy.

Knowledge is what I think we're talking about—internal knowledge about self. Knowledge about one's emotions and knowledge about knowledge about one's speculation and speculation capacities. What I'm trying to say is one's sense of who he is in relation to the entire world. . . That's not good either. Let me stop this for a moment and let me detour and refer back to some experience of mine as I grew up as a kid. I tend to think maybe some understanding of myself can come from when I was an adolescent and very unhappy because I didn't understand what life was; what I was, what the meaning of it all was.

Human cognition cannot be separated from the environment: family, social community, neighbors, technology. I think our nature is deeply social. We evolved in this very pronounced way through communication. It is used as reward and punishment. We go to jail if we violate a written language, the law. We are very enmeshed in our social life. Even if we sit in a cave for a week, we do not erase our interconnectedness to the human species.

It is possible to see ourselves, that which is not part of the external world, our own individuality, its own existence, its right to be individual. A creature totally separable from others. We can go into a reflective move; it can be helpful to develop new insights about ourselves. But in general, my everyday consciousness is very much tied up to what we have learned. I catch myself talking to myself. That is very much tied up to the way I grew up and used language.

A therapist can help others by recognizing how that person sees themself in the social world. I think there is something to be gained by introspection and dreaming. Perhaps, the core of our selves does not depend exclusively upon ties to the social world. There is a part of the self that is tied to the social world and a part that is separate from it. There is the social world mediated by language.

TC: I'd like to talk about what we can do to navigate the inner world without language. I come from a generation where we were exposed to a world with Japanese culture and are attracted to Eastern thought, religion. So, many American baby-boomers profess to a New-wave type thinking. What affected me was this parable:

A Master was viewing sunset with a disciple next to him, and the disciple spoke up and said, "That is a beautiful sunset," and the Master was silent. And they then went back to monastery and the disciple was told he can no longer go walking with the Master. He asked why and was told, "When you stood at the sunset, you did not experience the sunset. You experienced and admired your own words, not the experience itself." And that was considered a violation of the pure experience.

So, what do you think of the opinion of that Master?

JK: The Master was, in communicating with him why he would not walk with him, was teaching him. And at a later point I think the students who would learn from that teaching as opposed to if the Master had said nothing. Then he would not have helped develop this person's insight into the nature of the aesthetic experience devoid of language. I think that it is true, perhaps, that some of us, when we see a sunset or see a new thing such as a new animal that looks beautiful, we say, "Oh! You know, that's wonderful. I think it's great." We use words to talk about it and we label it because we believe it must be remembered. And those are utterances that only partially reflect the individual's internal experience that is independent of language.

And, one of the things that is helpful, I think, about our experiences in elementary school is that we are taught to draw things in first grade using coloring books and so on and we do this and it is done by verbal instruction as well as by our own direct experience. So, I guess what I'm saying is that, and I think is true is that, we do have our internal private experiences, whose origins are not tied to others such as our teachers, etc. But at the same time, we can only talk about those thinks, like you and I are talking—using words. And we can approximate what we're talking about which is a non-verbal entity.

I know the way to kind of stimulate that: I would imagine if you and I decided to do an experiment and just go with each other off to the hillside and just sit for a whole day just experiencing the world we could perhaps learn to do some fundamental private development. But. I think that that aspect alone is just a part of the fact that we are social creatures and the fact that language is necessary for the development of the individual, I think is quite evident. I cannot imagine any child growing up who has not been spoken to, who could become a great wise person who, sort of, has the inner knowledge that if somehow, we could tap, we would find remarkable development. I would think that would exist. I think that, I don't know, it's just you and I right now are exploring a realm of human existence. Which it sometimes seems to ring a bell and at times it sounds like, just irrelevant. But I daresay, our communication is vital for the further cultivation of this completely internal private kind of thing—the existence.

TC: Yes, it's a tangle.

JK: OK. So, anyway, you know, one of things I like about you, Tom, is that you have recognized the central issues about living and about personal happiness and so on in a way that very, very few others do. That's why I feel as though I am one of your kinfolks.

TC: It's an honor.

JK: It's a good feeling. It's something that I think people sometimes call "love." A shared sense of being in a world that has some great vitality from which we get a lot of energy and a sense of being a little bit more complete as individuals growing or becoming more human or whatever the hell it is, we become. It's a kind-of very important sort-of a thing. I've always recognized that part of your "self," which is kind of important.

Anyway, sometimes it might be worthwhile for us to develop methods of introspection aided by technology and we might be able to learn some things by talking with guys like Suduki Roshi, who is no longer alive. But, people like him who have meditated and developed a sense of wisdom that many have come to recognize. When he heard about what I was doing, he didn't comment with great excitement, but I think I could tell, he thought there was something about this, and about this Joe Kamiya, who is doing stuff that is related to what his concerns were. Perhaps because of the fact he had probably almost no training in biology and things like this, he, like everyone else, including me, assume our minds are our own. And we look into them but that they're not really related to our brains and our bodies. I think that in another way the intuitive people often talk about their bodies, but they don't often talk about their brains or their minds. What I would like to say is: Wouldn't it be interesting if we try to write about this?

TC: Absolutely. That's what we're doing [laughter]. That's what we're doing, Joe.

JK: OK. Because I think it would be a helpful thing to the world.

TC: Absolutely.

JK: OK, so I expect you to write the first six chapters and then I'll have a little summary of it. How would that be?

TC: Well, yes—Joe. You are very, very inspiring. To all of us.

The work would be focused on your work and contributions. I think the emphasis will be on how it inspires others to take hold of something which normally just floats right by. One of the analogies I use is of a fish who has no word for water because he doesn't know the difference. And while I agree that the use of language that gets us in very good stead, I think it allows us to circle the wagons around the prize. But the language does not get us the prize.

And I'm reminded of another Zen story of, again the Master, who had passed on the learning to his disciple who was now charged with enlightenment and the Master gives a large pile of papers to the student and says, "These are now yours to have." And the student immediately takes the papers to the fire and begins to burn them one at a time. And the Master is panic stricken. He runs to the student and says, "What are you doing here?" And the student turns calmly to the Master and says, "What are you saying here?"

Now we young naive white kids get a big kick out of these. But what I want to emphasize is that in the world after Joe Kamiya has arrived, we are learning about tools to explore the primacy of the inner world. And go where language cannot take us.

JK: I got started in my own work because, I think, I was interested in self-exploration. And I got started because it... happened while I was at the University of Chicago. I was still sometimes finding myself pondering some of the thoughts that I had when I was a kid of existence and what it was.

This discrimination training could go a long way to what we are talking about.

Suppose if I talk about myself and I develop a new sense of myself. Maybe I can find a way to track my discrimination training of myself. For example, I would like to know what happens when someone prays, what is the brain state of praying, or artists in the groove, or musicians when playing. Then we could create more knowledge of what is happening in the brain during these activities. Suppose I want to write poetry to express new ways of expression, possibly if I was monitoring the EEG and I had insight I might find there were states I was in and that would help me.

When you think about it, that will certainly be a treasured and valued activity known to be something quite a bit beyond writing poetry or playing different kinds of music. This has to do with looking at the way in which evolution and society, as it has evolved in evolution, has structured our internal, material world known as our neurons, and muscles, and stomachs, etc.

And this means that we are actually looking at the very base of our experience. And our vocabulary for experience can become much more refined because we would notice that the same kind of words had sometimes been used to describe quite different sorts of the internal experience or internal activity.

Anyway, this is what excites me—the whole world told by biofeedback in which we find ourselves in the middle of. Especially neurofeedback. Because now we're looking at the material processes known as the central nervous system that constitutes the base of human experience—the basic human experience.

CK: How is this the basis of human experience?

JK: By the human experience I mean the private world of the individual. And so, you know it's going to be exciting because almost every week we should begin to see some article or some finding by somebody in society: there are a good many societies being stimulated by our field code—called biofeedback—because, you know, it's good to start looking at the physiology and neurophysiology and laws of activity of the way neurons get together to create experience. And so, you know, I'm certainly hoping, and maybe with some good reason, expecting that the next 20, 30, 50 years you're going to see a very dramatic change in what we consider to be human knowledge.

TC: Look at the example of the thermometer. From it you get one simple reading, that everyone can agree upon. Suddenly, we get theories of heat and thermodynamics and the entire science of how heat and energy are related, and some of the most profound findings and laws. Including Fourier theory and analysis. And this then led to how entropy and statistics came, all from one simple measurement from a thermometer reading. It all came because we all agreed on one measurement. What can we do? We measure alpha waves & beta, coherence and synchrony.

I read a paper about consciousness, coherence and entropy. Sounds like we are discovering a thermometer that will move us through the brain. The paper is by

Guerrera, et al. We can do this with EEG. What about a measure that literally measures consciousness, what about that?

JK: We can get into confusions. But we can find agreements as we go along. Consciousness is a multi-meaning thing. At a certain level it's an understandable notion we say that man is unconscious or conscious or we say that this man has a different consciousness due to living in another country.

We can talk about it as something we are familiar with. But we can talk about concepts in common. Musicality, consciousness, have different meanings to different people, yet they have common agreement. But we have substantial individual meanings. Our side of psychophysiology will help to decrease confusion between these words. Poetry can benefit from what we say about neurophysiology. The notion of a marker is a substantial step forward in this regard.

JoK: Do you know about anyone doing research on the EEG of someone looking at ambiguous figures at the point at which they switch perceptions, or perception switch, things like that in embedded figures something that is discrete, like the woman and the vase thing, as an example.

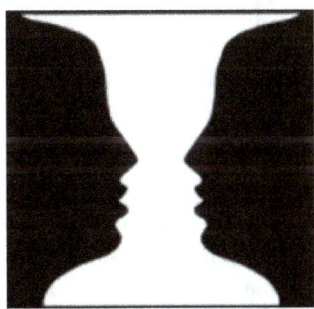

JK: Let me verbalize what you are talking about, it is like the ambiguous figures that can be seen in more than one way, and where his attention moves, and suddenly you see a different image where you can look at different perspectives of different possible perceptions of it—different ways of looking at it, reversible figures, like Necker Cubes and so on that have those properties, sometimes called illusions but they're not. They are very interesting switches of the mind and what Joanne is saying is that it is interesting to see what is and how it is happening in the brain when those switches in perception occur and I think that's a good one. It is precisely aimed at a phenomenon, it has the feel of a kind of importance for the future, because like when we think about particular issues, all of a sudden we get an insight into why, what we have been thinking about is a little bit misdirected, and a new insight is actually a more integrated insight; a more productive view appears And that kind of creative or productive thinking is something that there is very little research on. It would be very useful, I think, for a group such as the one I am fantasizing here, to get involved in investigating.

TC: One could not have imagined what has been accomplished over the two- and three-hundred years in the outer world. We've penetrated to the sub-atomic (sub-particle) level in the outer world. So, as we explore the inner world, what kinds of laws and physics are we going to discover?

JK: And we are only now beginning to find some strange things. And, by the way, one of the most intriguing possibilities, I believe, lies in the explicit formulation of quantum theory in relation to consciousness. As opposed to the standard classical physics we are dealing with a new concept of the fundamental particles of existence. And we are only now beginning to find some strange things. I think particle physicists and the people who are in the discussion of the Kubit, etc. of quantum are.

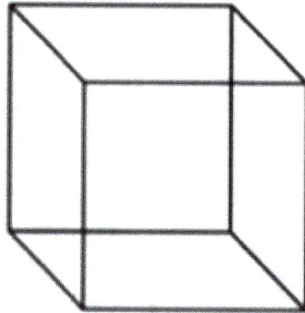

TC: I'm reading a book right now by Evan Harris Walker called *The Physics of Consciousness*. And on page 223, he explains that synaptic transmission of information is cloudy. It occurs at the level of electron tunneling so that it is a statistical quantum phenomenon. So, your brain is harnessing at the quantum level of information and it's staggering to realize that is not Newtonian. It's in a quantum world and it's statistical and cloudy.

JK: It sounds exciting, epic making if it occurs, if in our lifetime a new science of consciousness: the physics of consciousness.

TC: Yes, the neurophysics of consciousness.

JK: This is a highly developed conceptual area to clear up the relationship of primary observation of human consciousness and the description of the relationship which is a crucial step. I am glad you mentioned that, I didn't know it was going on. I have read quantum concepts and it's fascinating to see a real opening up of theory. I am wondering where folks like us could be gathered together either by phone or physical gathering to promote this kind of description.

TC: Yes, maybe something online is called for.

JoK: In the universe everything is conscious in one form or another.

JK: The whole damn topic of human consciousness is so important for scientific understanding that it's a bloody shame that we, especially we, as psychologists, have been really slow on the eight ball on that. And everyone, generally speaking, has. But, it's the scientific topic of all time.

TC: It is, isn't it?

JK: And it's because of the fact that it hinges on so many things that we think we are as human beings. It feels good to see interest awakening in this field. I feel fortunate that this is happening now. It is intuitively self-evident to all of us that a good science of consciousness would be enormously helpful because there are so many things about our own states of mind that we don't fully understand – we just live by them because that's what we have. Relating them, especially to the neurophysiology world. But not only that—also to the social world. This would be enormously helpful. I think we're going to see some very important changes occurring in what we teach for science.

There's no reason why we shouldn't start teaching this kind of stuff in elementary school. You know and getting people to understand that consciousness is a scientific subject very much like we study geography and history and physics and so on. I think we'll see important changes in teaching science that should be taught in elementary school, and should be just like history, English, etcetera.

The basic idea is that it's the use of the brain and body relationship to consciousness that will be richly rewarded. Because now we have a technology that would seem to be useful when that technology is feedback and know what to do. And of course, with using all of the advances in modern physiological and neurophysiological science so the notion of convergence, maybe taught in required courses, is basic to all science. That is to say areas of knowledge are related to each other. And the more clearly we become of how that relationship occurs, is the better off we are as sophisticated knowledgeable individuals not quite as blindly going ahead in life as we otherwise might.

I guess it's very easy to become overly personalized about this kind of stuff. But then the necessity of it evolves. Self-exploration tends to get wrapped up that way.

I was pontificating about what a great field this neurofeedback field is. And at some point, in our conversation I should like to go into that with you. And bore you or excite you.

CK: Please tell us why you think this is such a fantastic field.

JK: Well you know I think that first day was pure luck that you know I was just fumbling around with it and we began to realize that people can hear the sound of their brain waves by altering an audio device so that they can effectively hear one small function of the brain and that was back in the 60s and the field has developed substantially, of course, in the direction of therapy. Which is very good and that's what makes it possible for people to earn their livings as well as contribute to the science. But I think that there's something that needs further thought about the future of the science of this field and let me just, if you don't mind, let me ride along for perhaps three or four minutes in that direction.

TC & CK: Of course! Please go ahead.

JK: I believe that, to summarize what I'm going to say, is that substantial advances in the science of mind are going to be made possible by the neurofeedback technology. The reason is, perhaps best argued or illustrated by the writings of Kurt Lewin, a psychologist back in the late 30s or early 40s and 50s. He was prone to drawing diagrams of the self and of the objects of the self or the objects of perception.

You may recall in your undergraduate reading of Kurt Lewin's maps, and so on, the argument that he was making, that there was an important consideration of locating the self in the map of the cognitions of the individual. And to me that makes sense intuitively. I mean, we're always mapping our own welfare, or security, our dangers and threats etc., relative to the world, as we think about all our friends and enemies and neutral people and strangers and people that we love and people we hate.

And what I am thinking is that the improvement in imagery of brain process, which will go beyond simple EEG and topographic mapping of EEG functions, perhaps also with MRI and other imaging technology, that we will begin to see how, in brief, how the mind operates. And in slight expansion how the perceived self relates to the events in its world. And when you think about, like what we're talking about right now, I'm trying to make a point to two people about my thoughts. and my ego, or self, is represented in explaining this kind of thing to the people you come across.

So, now this is just a beginning statement of where we are in the science of this area because we have been, quite rightly, preoccupied with the clinical implications and utility of the neurofeedback. But I believe that the day is going to arrive when a theoretical reformulation of the mind body problem can take place and it's going to revolutionize what is being taught in courses in philosophy as well as in psychology because that field has always been concerned with the status of the mind and that will be a happy event because we will be able to go beyond what people were able to do just by talking to each other about it without the help of observations inside the body, especially in the brain.

And so that's my theme song for the future of neurofeedback. I am biased, of course, because having contributed to the development of it, working just from initial curiosity about maybe one might be able to detect and discern the presence of alpha activity in the EEG, it all kind-of began to grow like a snowball into a more substantial kind of movement in thought up of mine I guess and that's where I'm at now.

Unfortunately, I do not have a lab right now, and in a way, I suppose that's a good thing because that means a lot of hard work. It very often takes you away from theorizing and that kind of thing. But anyway, so that's the theme song for this morning and I think that I should stop at this point and talk about anything else that needs to be talked about this morning.

CK: Well I actually have a question around that to make sure I understand what you're saying. You're saying that we don't need to look at the brain. That a person's personal observations should be scientific enough. Is that what I'm hearing?

JK: No, that's not quite what I'm saying. I'm saying that it is terribly important for the person to be able to conceive and imagine and recognize without any neurophysiological help about what one's mind is with respect to the external world. Do I hate this person? Do I love him? Are my children behaving OK? I wish I could make more money because the tax function turned out blight, and so on. So, the self is represented in normal everyday thinking of everybody. And what I'm saying is that the next step in the development of the science of mind will actually help the phenomenological analysis because it will provide what is actually happening when our consciousnesses are functioning—that is to say our phenomenology is operating.

Our brains are doing it and to deny that is surely going to be a loser. So, we have begun to see, for example, that when someone is anxious his alpha will drop down substantially. We know for more sensory-simple things, when a person is imagining something or seeing something up close the alpha drops down.

Phase relationships change with some kinds of cognitive functions and I'm not an expert in that because I have not been following the experimental work in this field. But I am just, sort of, forecasting a bright future for this field because it will aid the process that you referred to, that is to say, the mental cognitive activity about what are our thoughts are doing, and what, who we are, etc. Because, let's face it, our thoughts are made possible by structures in the real world known as brains and bodies—that we know. And we have begun to catch glimpses of what's happening in the brain and body as we think, as we image, as we get angry, as we get afraid.

Way back in the 30s a beginning was made, though maybe even before, when the GSR was used to map fear and startle. That the beginning hinted quite clearly and strongly insisting that our phenomenology, our subjective experience, is tied into a very strict way with our bodies and brains. And that kind of insight or thought was not new, I'm sure. Plato must have thought of that too, even though he never even saw a brain perhaps. But we now have much more to go on. Plato and all of the philosophers and all of the Hindu and Chinese and Japanese Zen masters who have been strong using only the phenomenological analysis that they will now have something to help them. And I predict that a modern Zendo, which is a place where Zen is practiced, will now, also, have a little section where equipment is available for mapping what's happening in the brain as a person does things. And this may will be part of the instruction sequence of the masters when they are young beginners.

CK: Yeah, that's happening right now. Davidson has done work with disciples of the Dalai Lama, who is not even a closet neuroscientist. He appreciates neuroscience a great deal.

JK: So that's right. The Dalai Lama has been one of the encouragers of this whole scientific approach to the psychology and mental activity of the human being. That's encouraging—very much so.

It certainly seemed to me that many of us who call ourselves liberals ought to get off our asses and write more contributions to our mass media or daily papers or magazines and editorials and the like. One sees very little of that. One sees grousing—like I am doing. But your question is a good one. I think one thing that might be helpful is for people to discuss what each of us could do that would make a difference. And certainly, it seems to me that writing into the editorial and commentary mass media will be of help and being sure to get our voices heard. And where there are televised or radio broadcasts of opinions about social issues.

I think that many of us, kind of, hold back and just sort of grouse about the fact that the Republican party is dominated by so many conservatives and that beyond that grousing we don't do much. I would like to express this view that I should myself take pen in hand and get on the phone and call and do things that get reflected into the mass media.

I think the point of view of the highly conservative Republican view is really fairly small in number. But it can be made much less popular and much more disliked by the population in general by more of us speaking out and in whatever way would be effective. I certainly can do more of it myself. We have been kind of quiet complainers but without really effectively doing something about it.

TC: Yes well, I think that's a very realistic and important point of view. Are you suggesting you're going to write something? Joanne? Are you and Joe going to put something out?

JoK: I don't know. This putting out follows up articulating one's point of view in the first place. In other words, I'm not going to look for a publisher until I have something to say. But I feel that one way we contribute to the quality of life around us is by being thoughtful and kind to others. The idea of America First—it makes me cringe you know. Not that I'm not OK with being an American. But "me first," that's never been a particularly salubrious way to conduct life. You know like, "Get out of my way. I'm here."

TC: Yeah. I understand. But we do see people who seem to really respond to that. So, I think we need to contemplate how we got there. How we got to this point and maybe it's inevitable. Maybe the population has to have a certain number of people who are going to, kind of, be these ultra—I'll call them preservatives. They're not just conservatives they want to preserve.

JoK: They're opposite of being conservative. They're destructive.

TC: Yeah, they want to freeze things out and they want to get the other guy you know. So, I think you raise some very, very good points. Somehow, we have created a society in which there was enough people worried about you know a lot of things which may or may not have needed worrying about. That they put someone in charge who is very, very clear. I mean you're withdrawing from international agreements and cancelling Protection Acts and by cutting down the Department of Education cutting down the Environmental Protection I mean maybe these things were too big. I don't know maybe they weren't as effective as they should have been but the message that's going out is that they're not of sufficient value and we're going to cut and then put nonscientists in charge of scientific type jobs. This appears to be what everybody wanted. I shouldn't say this is what everybody wanted. No, I shouldn't say that. I should say that enough people wanted, or thought they wanted, or maybe they didn't know what they wanted. But they got it.

Chapter 11

Thinking Inside the Box

When I see X in my box, several things else are happening, especially in the body and brain, that others can see and we learn quite quickly that Lo and behold that box contains many, many secrets that we are beginning to unearth and have a long ways to go yet.

JK: You know the whole damn topic of human consciousness is so obviously important for scientific understanding that it's a bloody shame that we, especially we psychologists, have been really slow on the 8 ball on that. And every book, generally speaking, has, but it's the scientific, (in my opinion) the scientific, topic of all time. You know because of the fact that consciousness impinges on so many things that we think we are as human beings. And it's just so good to see interest awakening in this field. I feel extremely fortunate that it is right now. You know it's funny that its intuitively self-evident to all of us that a good science to consciousness would be enormously helpful because there are many things about our own states of mind that we don't fully understand. We just live them because that's what we have. But relating them, especially to the neurophysiology world—and not just to that, but also to the social world, will be enormously helpful. I think we're going to see some very important changes occurring in what we teach for science. There's no reason why we shouldn't start teaching this kind of stuff in elementary school. Getting people to understand consciousness as a scientific subject should be very much like how we study geography and history and physics and so on.

TC: Well, let me let me throw something at you that I put on social media about five years ago. I'd like to revisit it and it is from the *Philosophical Investigations of Wittgenstein* and in paragraph 293 he says, "Suppose everyone had a box with something in it and will call it a beetle. No one can look in anyone else's box. And everyone says he knows what a beetle is only by looking at *his* beetle. And we would quite possibly have something very different in everybody's box. But suppose the word beetle had a different use in different languages. So, it would not be used as the name of a thing. It would be used to name what everyone thinks is in their box. The box might even be empty."

JK: That's wonderful. In a certain way, I suppose, that's exactly what we do—we look into our empty boxes. But we know that can't be true because we know that we can still have room to argue and dispute and be able to point to certain things that occur—first off of course, with relation to all the other events in body and brain. We know of the various many correlates so that when we say, "When I see X in my box," several things else are happening, especially in the body and brain, that others can see and we learn quite quickly that Lo and behold that box contains many, many secrets that we are beginning to unearth and have a long ways to go yet. That's in the physiologic world. But I think also with respect to what that little thing is that we're calling "little," or whatever, is also paralleled by certain behaviors that we do, like we say when we say, "Ouch" or when we cry with tears or when we laugh. Those have their concomitance in what's happening in the box too. And so, when I see Cindy crying, I know without her telling me, that inside her box there is something that we call "sad." And so, in a way the box idea, presented as you read it to me, has a certain appeal. But we know that curiously that box is not secret.

What I see in my box, you see also because of the way I behave and because of the way my body works, which you can detect if you have me hooked up to something. So anyway, it's a good kind of question to put forth as a puzzle for classes in consciousness. It's a good reminder of the complexities that we have about understanding our own consciousness.

TC: I think it's an interesting analogy. Your comments make me wonder what if I could see the reflection in your eyes as you look in your box.

JK: Ha-ha. Well if you could, you could see how my pupils dilate—or not—depending on what I'm seeing. As I understand it, if I see what's inside it scares me. You would see dilation in my pupils. Whereas if other things were calming or have other emotional correlates you would see that change also. So, the eyes do show something from just examining other people's eyes because they happen to be part of the body's system that does experiencing. But it is, of course, a much more limited kind of source of information. It is in many respects not very informative. That's speculative of course because you know no one is the exacting measure of how that pupil dilates in the course of an individual's, let's say, self-reporting of events. It might be quite interesting in fact for that question to be explored.

But then there are other things about pupil dilation I suppose—about eyes. Perhaps some kind of stare-sort-of-look. And of course, the merriment that that causes the eyes to partially close when one laughs or is happy or whatever else that may happen. Those do tell a story about what's in that box or how they react to it.

CK: I have so many questions. If we have these boxes and we, ourselves, don't know what's in them, then how do we react when we open our own box? Rather than looking at how people react, you know and trying to figure out by looking at the physiological shift in their pupils. So, what about the visceral? What about the experience of that?

JK: That, of course, is where our specialty, as the British would say, comes in and that is biofeedback and neurofeedback: monitoring of the pupillary diameter or the whatever else the eyes can show objectively with instrumentation. That will certainly help fill the question of what's in the box. Of course, it's quite limited. But, I think we would still have to go largely on say, such that when I say what's my box there will be many, many things that I am reporting which I feel, but which are not being shown as correlates either in my behavior or in my physiologic mechanisms.

CK: But what about the emotion of it? The feeling of it?

JK: Well that is something—you certainly cannot feel how I feel.

CK: I'm not sure. You really believe that?

JK: In a way it is true. It's a good question, Cindy, because we could talk to each other about this subject if for some reason we did not have a sufficiently common experiential background to do so. And the fact that we are seemingly talking are, in fact, talking about the same subject, is a triumph of human evolution. It's incredible that we can do that, but we are doing it. And the reason we have learned to do it, I think, is by observing behavior at first. You know ever since we're children, when Mother scolds us and she is really mad, we know it. As opposed to when she scolds us when she's only moderately mad because of the way she behaves. And we learn through these correlates that Mama is an experiencing person, just as I am an experiencing person. So that's the marvelous thing. You and I and Tom have learned in a common verbal world some of the things inside these boxes of ours. In each of our boxes and dare to say, I am inside your box, Cindy. Whether you like it or not.

All: Ha, ha

CK: And I think that that's true and we're more sensitive to it when we're near each other even if it is just by the telephone. And where we are standing is the collective consciousness. . . energy, however you want to define it, that keeps us close to each other even when we're not.

JK: That's right. Yeah. And it's one of the most remarkable and wonderful things about life. It's terrific.

And you know what we're talking about is (I'm going to bring up an earlier thing we talked about) that's really worth writing about or having written about. People can become more appreciative of our marvelous inner boxes. I am mindful of what we said earlier, you know, that the science of experience, by which I mean the science of subjective experience, is a field waiting eagerly to be advanced ever since we have observed in psychiatric clinics and in clinical psychological clinics, etc., about behavior – verbal behavior especially, and what's happening inside the box is revealed by those interactions to the next party—the therapist, about what's in the patient's box and otherwise they could not be successful therapy processes. And the fact that it does work is good.

But at the same time, I think we can also, in some cases, delude ourselves into thinking we understand something when perhaps we don't. I can't think of any particular examples except maybe talking about superstitions that we sometimes generate amongst each other.

CK: Or cognitive dissonance or some other thing that we somehow shift to because we think that that is the thing that is going to keep us stable.

JK: The remarkable thing is that these qualities—these correlates—of what's inside each of our boxes, is that which makes it possible for us to talk to each other about what's inside that box.

So anyway, you know what we're doing right now—the three of us, is really a terribly important thing, that is what I would call, "the development of the science of consciousness" and it would be so important to get some of these things expressed in ways that others can add to it and join in it. And what we're talking about is the development of a body of literature: a book, a series of articles, and it can be done. And you and I and Tom and several others can be at the forefront developing a literature—a textual material. Initially it can be by verbal talking like we do, but eventually to become really effective, we need to get it down. Do you agree?

TC & CK: Absolutely, yes!

JK: OK. So, you know the next question is how do we go about doing that? Or how do we begin etc., etc. And certainly, I have to say that the books that Tom sent me will go a long way toward getting me started. I don't know if all three of us are up on top of those particular books. I have this say it'll take me at least a couple of weeks to get myself up to speed on those. But that would certainly be one way to begin is to comment on what is being written about by others or at least for us to show an awareness such that we don't sound like we were just repeating what many others have just said.

TC: Yes. I think we can come up with some original thinking. Joe you are the original thinker. You know 50 years ago in how we can explore the internal experience, the internal world, and these conversations are getting us to think about how we might be able to construct some interesting thought experiments, literally. And, thought experiment typically means I just sit and think about a problem and I come up with an answer. But I'm talking about doing experiments in thought.

JK: Experiment what with?

TC: Thoughts.

JK: Thoughts? Like in T-H-O-U-G-H-T-S?

TC: Yes. We want to do experiments where the manipulandum, the various variables are, in fact, thoughts. One thing that came to mind to me just now talking about the beetles and your interesting commentary: here's a thought experiment for you. The three of us are sitting at a table. Each of us has in front of us one dish of ice cream. So, there are three dishes of ice cream. They look the same. It's clear and white and each of us may or may not have the same type of ice cream. But they look the same. And we each take a taste. So, I taste my ice cream and you taste yours. And then Cynthia tastes hers. Now what can we do to begin to understand what it is we've experienced? And can we learn whether or not two of us have the same flavor?

JK: Yes, well—what we do is very simple, Tom. I'll give you a spoonful of mine and you hand me a spoonful of yours. And I'll share mine with Cindy.

TC: You're not allowed. You're not allowed to share the ice cream.

CK: Even so: I mean, vanilla tastes different to me than it does to you.

TC: So that's where I'm going with this is. I don't know if they are the same. How do we know they taste the same? Even if we have the same?

JK: When you say vanilla—when you say, "This tastes like vanilla," what that tells me is that you are from the same culture and you know what we're doing. I know because you've been brought up with the same language I have been. I am able to approximately get my own private sensation of vanilla. I would guess that therefore when you taste my ice cream it'll taste very much like yours and would say, "You know, we're eating the same flavor and it's called vanilla." Even though, initially the ice cream is put in front of each of us and we've only tasted that one, at this point, we are unsure of what the other person is eating. But fortunately, we have developed a communication system such that when you tell me that, "Oh, this tastes like vanilla." I know approximately what you mean. Just like when you say, "Ooh, that was a very embarrassing comment," I know what you mean.

I know what you mean when you say, "That made me mad." I know what you mean when I say, "Well, gee I don't know what you mean." I know roughly what you mean and that's the beauty of the fact that we have common neurophysiologically-based experiences that allow us, through our behaviors, to communicate about our private experiences. That is terrific.

TC: Let me dissent briefly. Because I have a client, who I worked with yesterday: a young man who has a lot of problems and he told me about a very significant problem in his life. And then he grinned and giggled and laughed and I said, "This is not funny. Why are you smiling and giggling? Aren't you angry?" And he said, "Yes, I'm angry." And then he laughed some more. How am I to know what's really going on with this person.

JK: Well obviously, at least to me, is that he had a recognition of how his emotionality has come to be seen in a new light because of the transactions he's had with his therapist. And it's a piece of insight. It is so wonderful that he laughs. It's sort of like, "Oh my God." Or, "I'll be damned." "Gee Wizz" kind of recognition of things that are going on. That's how I would interpret that. I mean how would you interpret that, Cindy?

CK: Well I don't know that we can interpret it based upon what Tom has only told us. I think it could be that that he identifies with what happened. We don't know whether the event was something that he did that he is embarrassed by, or that he is a sociopath and enjoyed it, or it was something that somebody else did. I don't think we have enough information to answer that other than just our visceral experience around what Tom was saying and our, sort of, our hit on this person because now we are closer to this person just based upon Tom's discussion about him.

JK: Well, OK. You know, it's kind of a remarkable thing—this thing called language applied to the private emotions. And thoughts and feelings, etc. that we do. And we do it apparently reasonably well. But then there are often times when we don't. And so, we are faced with the challenge of how can we improve upon that? And, that's the kind of thing that remains, I think, for the challenge.

It occurs to me that one of the things that we are doing is getting to know each other better. Perhaps more through this discussion than, perhaps, any other because we're exchanging words to represent the private experiences that we have comparing them and responding to them and talking about it.

We are developing a common base of meaning that didn't occur before these phone calls started. And I think it's marvelous. It's the way we humans work—by establishing a common ground of feeling. At least if I have a sense of sharing a common quest with Cynthia Kerson and Tom Collura. And I know they tend to share the same with me because of the way they're talking. And this is a remarkable triumph of human development and I'm, kind of, blown away by it.

TC: Joe, you know what I'm feeling right now is what is called "enouement," which is French. Are you ready for this?

JK: I'm ready.

TC: It is "the bittersweet feeling of having arrived in the future, seeing how things have turned out, but not being able to tell your past self."

JK: I see.

CK: That's interesting.

TC: There are many such words. If you look for them, you'll find them. Feelings you may not even realize you had but, with the word, now you know there's a feeling there.

JK: Could you spell that word that you used?

TC: Certainly: e-n-o-u-e-m-e-n-t.

And isn't it interesting how learning a new word can teach you that an emotion exists.

JK: Yes! Very good.

CK: I don't know that I've ever experienced that emotion to be honest. I'd have to really think about it. I don't know that I have that emotion or that I can experience that.

TC: Correct. So that's a thought experiment.

CK: Right. So that's a really interesting dialogue about the parallel entities of emotion and thought and how we have become so, you know, frontal lobed and so it's become so necessary for us to be social in this way that I wonder is it a curse? You know? Are we moving too fast? Are we moving away from intuition and sensitivity and emotion and moving too far into our frontal lobes?

TC: Right. And there are people who think that might be the case.

JK: OK. So, I'd prefer to go to other places in my brain and maybe even down into my body. And with Cynthia there, I'm prepared to go all the way down into the gonads.

TC: My heavens!

CK: I don't know how to take that. Let's not put that in the book, OK?

JK: It's a supreme complement. So anyway, it's wonderful what words can do.

CK: I do think that that's where pathology lie—often in that way we respond to things in our frontal lobes and don't allow ourselves the time (and I'm guilty of this, Lord knows) at times that we don't allow ourselves to experience the emotion or the feeling before we take action.

TC: And that's something I teach clients and I'm sure you do too, Cynthia. You want to teach them to experience an emotion and evaluate it so that, instead of reacting, they make a decision. And I've told my clients that emotions are just a behavior—are a decision.

CK: I don't know that an emotion is a decision. I think every emotion viscerally is the same whether you're upset or whether you're, you know, joyous. Your heart beats faster and you know and all the other physiological things but it's our brains that tell us what the emotion is like you just gave us that word and said, "Now we have a name. So that must mean that we have all had that emotion." Just because we have a name that must mean that we've had that emotion.

TC: It means somebody had it.

CK: It kind-of sounds a little bit like Déjà vu.

TC: Yes, that's another one. You know there are languages that don't have words for certain emotions.

CK: Right. And is that because they don't need to have them or more because people don't feel the emotion.

TC: Right. I don't know. Well we've already learned you can learn the name of an emotion that you've had but didn't have a name for.

JK: But you know I suspect that because of the fact that we are of the same species we have very common experience. We share very similar, if not identical, experiences even though we don't communicate with each other about them. I think for example if I meet someone from a different country—a different culture—in a different set of social behaviors, as I reach to shake hands with that party I already have a sense of communication and he has one because we already know that we are there for the purpose of enhancing our experience of each other and enjoying it. And so, we have that common sense (provided that we have been socialized properly and we're not, you know, psychopathic).

And so, this is what holds the whole country together—the whole world together, in so far as we sense the shared emotionality and value for our experiences. So that's what ties us together and leads us to hope for improvements in areas with people who we don't know, and or whatever. I think that the fact that we're talking by telephone means that we're almost sitting across a table from each other with the noticeable deficiencies compared to the table situation but at the same time we're accomplishing a hell of a lot just by talking. It's a remarkable thing. And that's what I'm saying Tom Collura, Cynthia Kerson and Joe Kamiya ought to put together a book with words that would help convey what we're trying to do.

CK: Well? What is it that we're trying to do? We are putting a book together; Joe and you bring that up every time. We're recording all of these conversations and we're intending to put them to pen. So, you have to remember that. Joanne you'll have to keep reminding him about that. What would we be accomplishing? What exactly would be our goal and what would we accomplish by publishing this book?

JK: That's great. Thank you for reminding me. We're writing a book and even though we're not aware that we were doing so.

I can think of ways that we can stimulate ourselves and others on to further experiential sharing of thoughts feelings, emotions, and that area of thoughts—in particular our thoughts about the world and the state of the world—part of it and I think that it's clear to me that much of the problems we have in our relations with each other is that we have not developed our sociality as nearly to the degree that we should. And especially with people from other countries and worlds. What we need is an international network which sometimes is called the Web or the Internet. You get people talking to each other about these things. It's a little bit hard without vocal communication.

So that's the end of my thought. I think it's what we're touching on some pretty damn important features about being human and I'm very glad for our conversation. It stimulates me to be thinking about what we talked about and curiously it helps bring forth many of the much earlier thoughts that I had as a adolescent about what life was all about and so on. And it's therefore very meaningful to me personally in more ways than I can express. It's this direct tying together one's own past experience with what's currently happening that is, I think, enlightening. At least I think I'm getting enlightened by these conversations.

TC & CK: Yes, we are.

JK: It's great. I love you both.

CK: So that's our purpose for publishing this book. Ultimately it is to open up the conversation; to engage people more in identifying with themselves emotionally rather than cognitively. Would you say that?

JK: Well, you guys are magic. You are stirring all kinds of wonderful feelings and thoughts especially thoughts about sensing.

TC: So, I think maybe we are all feeling a little "ellipsism." You want to know what that is?

JK & CK: Sure.

TC: Ellipsism is the sadness of knowing that you'll never be able to know how history will turn out.

CK: Oh? Is that the opposite of the other word?

TC: Oh, it's just one of many. I posted a link on our little page. There are so many words that you never knew. Here's another interesting one. Cynthia, you and Joe will enjoy this. Have you ever been in a hotel after a big meeting and everything is empty? And everything is quiet and you remember that the day before all your colleagues and friends were bustling around but now it's empty and quiet?

And I've told Terri when that happens, I say I always love being at the hotel the day after the conference. And there's a word for that. It's called "canopsia." It's called the "eerie forlorn atmosphere of a place that's usually bustling with people but is now abandoned and quiet."

CK: However, there's still things going on in there. There's the next conference that's energy is consumed in space. And so, I don't know if I like that.

TC: So, we need yet another word.

CK: Do we need another word? Do we really need another word? Can we just experience it without defining it?

TC: Now you're talking. That's the key. You probably could invent words forever.

CK: Yeah exactly and you'll be so distracted by inventing words that you're not having life. Like the photographer behind the camera.

TC: Good insight.

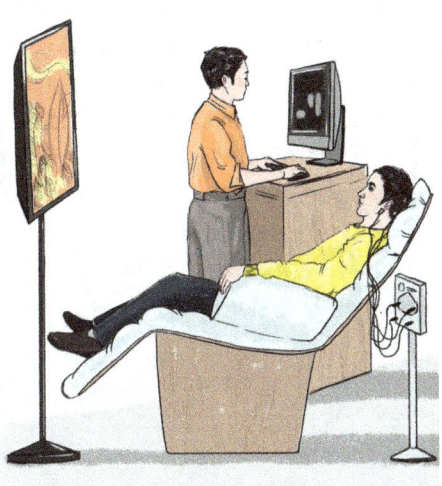

Chapter 12

The EEG, QEEG, and Biofeedback

Isn't it incredible that [QEEG] has not become a central tool for neurologists?

TC: Let's talk about EEG, and I hope we're also going to talk about QEEG and neurofeedback—not just using an EEG in a hospital to help a patient who has had a stroke or an injury or some such.

The medical aspect has just proven itself you know for almost a hundred years at this point that the EEG is a gold standard way to identify injury and reactions to malformations such as tumors, strokes, head injuries, toxic problems, such as hepatic encephalopathies and such. There is very, very strong acceptance in the medical community for EEG, primarily through visual inspection. Very little if any computer analysis is used in medicine, with the exception of seizure detection and detection of epileptiform abnormalities, such as spikes and sharp waves. So, the medical profession is using the EEG as an indicator when things are severely dysfunctional, disregulated, or just damaged.

Now the use of EEG, first of all with computers to, for example, measure alpha waves or now we measure beta waves, delta waves, we measure coherence and all these things. That branch is much less accepted by the medical community and it, sort of, has a world of its own which is quantitative EEG and the American Neurological Association, for example, has published a position paper that this is not reliable or useful for head injuries, concussions or any of this kind of stuff.

JK: But do they acknowledge that it has some utility for some people?

TC: They indicate that it might be a useful adjunct. But only in cases where the visual inspection of the EEG indicates the abnormalities. So, sure, they agree that you might be able to use a quantitative EEG to localize or quantify some abnormality.

JK: It's interesting to me why they don't read the book, which is called *The Future of the Mind*, which is a number 1 best seller by Michio Kaku. Unfortunately, he also does not even mention neurofeedback or EEG.

TC: Now this is interesting that you mention that Joe because I have spoken with Michio Kaku. In fact, he even got his hands on a BrainMaster at one point. He bought one more than 10 years ago and gave it to his daughter to play with. But I do believe that his fascination or interest in EEG waned. I will make a comment Joe, that for the past 30 or 40 years everytime I go into a bookstore and I find a book that talks about consciousness or the brain or the mind or anything like this, I always go back to the index and I flip through it and I see if EEG even appears and what you find is that it generally does not. Even Norman Doidge, in his book, *Change Your Brain; Change Your Mind*, which is an excellent book, doesn't say much of anything about EEG—maybe a half a page.

JK: I find that fascinating.

TC: It is fascinating; I don't find it discouraging. To me it tells me we're still pioneers.

JK: What I also suspect is that people, especially neurologists are actually threatened by the fact that using neurofeedback is actually effective in treating certain kinds of ailments. It's an economic —I suspect that's part of reason they put it down, because it threatens their own livelihood.

TC: Well it does. It actually also threatens psychologists -what we're finding. But one thing I want to get to before we dig too deep into what's not there is to is to make you aware there is a thriving and large community of QEEG practitioners. Tens of thousands of people are using QEEG. They just don't happen to be doctors. They are usually either forward-thinking psychologists but also a very wide range of professionals, including social workers, mental health counsellors, nurses, psychiatric practitioners, and many non-medical people, are using QEEG, for example race car drivers, professional sport, football, baseball. We see these players using QEEG and then neurofeedback.

JK: Isn't in incredible that it has not become a central tool for neurologists?

TC: For seizures and such. No, not QEEG at all. Probably less than 10 percent of neurologists have even heard of QEEG.

JK: That's really, really remarkable.

TC: And I'll tell you I was at the Cleveland Clinic for eight years. So that put me on the inside, not counting the years in graduate school as an engineer. And they view QEEG as being rather imprecise and not of value because they say there are so many different ways you can try to interpret a color map. And the neurologists really stay with visual inspection. And let me tell you, Joe when I teach QEEG, we teach several days of visual inspection of the EEG, in addition to using computers. We do not abandon the use of EEG. But the mainstream EEG community is focused on epilepsy, concussions, and other types of disorders.

However, what's encouraging is this entirely different world has popped up. And there's two worlds. One is the world of quantitative EEG, which is loaded with psychologists, and engineers, and mental health professionals of all types. But then another world of neurofeedback, which again has probably hundreds of thousands now of practitioners—many of whom do not look at QEEG, but they just do neurofeedback. So, it's sort of like you know pop music. I look at the world of popular music. You've seen this go by in your lifetime—how different traditions and different genres spring up almost out of nowhere. For example, when I was a kid the big deal was rock n roll. And my parents said, "Oh no—rock n roll. It's nonsense." Well, by the time I was out of college it wasn't just rock n roll. There were six kinds of rock n roll. There was hard rock, there was soft rock; there was heavy metal; there was country rock; there was folk rock.

JK: I ask this question: Has a study been done to find out if the inspection of the raw EEG can reveal things which the QEEG cannot.

TC: Yes. The answer is yes. The QEEG does not accurately reflect the morphology of the wave forms—the shapes of the wave forms for example. So, if you have a very irregular type of theta wave for example the QEEG might not differentiate that from a more regular type of theta which would have two different medical consequences. And the QEEG does not reflect rare events in any useful way. So, by visual inspection you might find a very abnormal but relatively rare event such as an epileptic spike or an absence seizure. And if these are rare then the QEEG will not reveal them. And so yes there are a few very, very important things. The QEEG does not reveal the shapes and distributions of the EEG. There's a visual sense you get by looking at an EEG that's different from what you get from the QEEG.

Now in converse there are things the QEEG reveals that the visual inspection may not see, may miss. For example, if the alpha waves are let's say 50 percent higher than normal, you might not visualize it. You might say, "Oh gee, that's a nice-looking alpha wave." But the QEEG would tell you, "Oh, but the average amplitude over here is 12μV or something." So, the QEEG is good for that and also connectivity activity. The QEEG can reveal what we call coherence, and phase.

So, we use them hand in hand and frankly what we do in my lab and what I teach people: by looking at the EEG you try to predict what the QEEG will reveal. If the QEEG reveals what you expected, you take that as confirmatory. If the QEEG reveals new information that you didn't expect, then you take that as sort of a revelation, new information, and bring them together. There are cases where the QEEG gives information which can be misleading.

JK: Sure. Now comes the next question: Is it not feasible nowadays with much increased computer power and economy of computation that some of the rare things that can be seen visually could be detected by special programs. I should think so. If you could see it, it should be detected by a computer.

TC: Sure. Seizure detections and spike detectors do that. So, an epileptologist would be very likely to use a spike detector. And that's a piece of software that might use joint time frequency analysis (JTFA) or some of these other arcane mathematical methods that you're alluding to such—as homomorphic decomposition independent components analysis, principal components analysis, etc. Absolutely yes. Computers can be used to spot these rare events. But that's not in the domain of QEEG. That's in the domain of clinical epileptology and computer-assisted analyses because then the physician will always go back to the visual inspection of the waveforms.

JK: Sure. But I should think that at some point it can be reached where anybody who is outfitted with QEEG ought to be able to, through modification of his program be able to see epileptiform or any other abnormality that is visually recognizable—even if it would require a second run through some of the postings made, it would be possible. So that does not have to depend upon visual inspection at all. I should think at some point it would become a superior method of detecting, as opposed to visual detection, which depends on the alertness of the operator.

TC: I would speculate that probably 90 percent of epileptologists do use computer-assisted spike and seizure detection. That's very common. But that's not in the domain of QEEG. Certainly, you can go buy a system that will do both. You run one piece of software and it will detect spikes and seizures and such and you run another piece of software and you'll get maps and such. And sure, I would imagine a very small minority of neurologists are actually doing both and they do find it helpful.

JK: Let me say, I think it is very important for those of us right now, all four of us and dozens of others like us to begin developing simple training materials, simple examples. Perhaps not starting with the EEG but starting with something simple like the skin potential or the skin resistance changes. And developing little lesson manuals:

1. How to attach the electrodes.

2. Turning on the equipment

3. What the equipment consists of, etc.

And then you have them hooked up and then you say "Boo" and the child sees a tremendous rise with a 1-second delay in his skin potential or skin resistance and that is the thing that really captivates the interests of everybody. And it won't be long before the kids will be refusing to go out to recess to instead play around with the equipment and say things that embarrass each other or etc.

The exploratory mood is activated by the biofeedback systems and that's the perfect reason why I think there will be a great future, by the way, commercially in the development of teaching materials and equipment for public education. That's an area you might give some serious thought to, Tom.

TC: Yes. Absolutely.

JK: It could be fairly simple process also.

CK: You have some wonderful ideas about public schools and the possibility of educational biofeedback. There is much to accomplish from these ideas with a more modern perspective.

JK: Right. Yes. It was my feeling that the technology, particularly for all forms of feedback would be extremely useful to introduce as part of a child's educational development. Because here the person can do that kind of self-exploration that the technology would permit by simply asking questions. And that child could begin to start using it as a kind of diary of ideas that he might ask about things.

I guess what I'm thinking about is when I was a teenager as we've already discussed. If I had these tools back then, I may have been able to understand my emotions and not spend so much time pondering about things that may have held me back in my own personal growth. I imagine if kids were given these tools now, we might spare many of them my experience.

Joe's Publications

Some personality correlates of tachistoscopic self-recognition
  Joe Kamiya
  Ph. D. Thesis dissertation, University of California Library, Berkeley, 1954

Behavioral, Subjective, and Physiological Aspects of Drowsiness and Sleep
  Joe Kamiya
  Functions of Varied Experience, Chapter 6, Dorsey Press, 1961, PP 145-174

Learned EEG Alpha Wave Control by Humans
  Joe Kamiya, Dennis Zeitlin
  Report Number 183, 1963, California Department of Mental Hygiene, Research Division pp 1-12

Conscious Control of Brain Waves
  Joe Kamiya
  Psychology Today, April 1968, pp 57-60

Electrophysiological Studies of Dreaming as the Prototype of a New Strategy in the Study of Consciousness
  Johann Stoyva and Joe Kamiya
  Psychological Review, 1968, Vol. 75, No 3, pp 192-205

Visual Evoked Reponses in Subjects Trained to Control Alpha Rhythms
  Kamiya J, Callaway E, Yeager CL.
  Psychophysiology, Vol 5., No. 6, 1969, pp 683-695

Biofeedback and Self-Control: (Preface)
  Joe Kamiya
  Aldine Annual, 1970, pp ix-xvi
  Aldine-Atherton, Chicago–New York

Biofeedback
  Joe Kamiya, Joanne Gardner Kamiya
  Aldine Annual, 1970, pp 115-125
  Aldine-Atherton, Chicago–New York

Operant Conditioning of Stomach Acid pH.
  Paul Gorman and Joe Kamiya
  Read before the Biofeedback Research Society Meeting, Boston, 1972

Abdominal-thoracic respiratory movements and levels of arousal
  Beverly Timmons, Joseph Salamy, Joe Kamiya, Dexter Girton
  Psychonomic Science, September 1972, Volume 27, Issue 3, pp 173–175

Posterior Alpha-Wave Characteristics of Eidetic Children
    Charles J. Furst, Joanne Gardner, Joe Kamiya
    Psychophysiology, Volume 11, Issue 5, September 1974, pp 603–606

Observation of very slow potential oscillations in human scalp recordings
    G Girton, Dexter & Benson, Kathleen & Kamiya, Joe
    Electroencephalography and Clinical Neurophysiology. 35., 1974, pp 561-568

A Very Stable Electrode System for Recording Human Scalp Potentials with Direct-Coupled Amplifiers
    Dexter G Girton and Joe Kamiya
    Electroencephalography and Clinical Neurophysiology, 1974, 37, pp 85-88

Conflicting Results in EEG Alpha Feedback Studies: Why Amplitude Integration Should Replace Percent Time
    James V. Hardt and Joe Kamiya

Applied Psychophysiology and Biofeedback
    March 1976, Volume 1, Issue 1 pp 63-75

Methodological issues in alpha biofeedback training
    Sonia Ancoli and Joe Kamiya
    Biofeedback and Self-regulation
    June 1978, Volume 3, Issue 2, pp 159–183

Autoregulation of the EEG Alpha Rhythm: A Program for the Study of Consciousness,
    Joe Kamiya
    Mind/Body Integration: Essential Readings in Biofeedback, pp 289-297
    Springer, 1979

Joe Kamiya
    Chapter 10, pp 127-138
    Psychologie im Gespräch
    Richard I. Evans, Editor
    Springer, 1979

Biofeedback and behavioral medicine 1979/80: therapeutic applications and experimental foundations
    David Shapiro; Johann Stoyva; Joe Kamiya; et al
    Aldine Publishing Company, 1981

The Nature of Respiratory Changes Associated with Sleep Onset.
  Karen Naifeh & Joe Kamiya
  Sleep 4(1):49-59 · February 1981

Discrimination of Sleep Onset Stages: Behavioral Responses and
  Verbal Reports
  Elizabeth Gibson, Franklin Perry, Dana Redington, and Joe Kamiya
  Perceptual and Motor Skills, 1982, 55, pp 1023-1037

Biofeedback of alveolar carbon dioxide tension and levels of arousal
  Karen H. Naifeh, Joe Kamiya, D. Monroe Sweet
  Biofeedback and Self-Regulation 7(3):283-99, October 1982

On the Relationships Among Subjective Experience, Behavior, and Physiological
  Activity in Biofeedback Learning
  Joe Kamiya
  Chapter from, Self-Regulation of the Brain and Behavior, pp.245-254
  Springer, 1984

General automatic components of motion sickness
  Suter, Steve & Toscano, Bill & Kamiya, J & Naifeh, K.
  National Aeronautics and Space Administration, Ames Research Center, Moffett
  Field, California 1985

General Autonomic Components of Motion Sickness
  Cowings, Patricia & Suter, Steve & Toscano, Bill & Kamiya,
  Joe & Naifeh, Karen
  Psychophysiology. 23. pp 542-51. 1986

Four Congenitally Blind Children with Circadian Sleep-Wake Rhythm Disorder
  H. Naifeh, Karen & W. Severinghaus, John & Kamiya, Joe
  SLEEP. 10. 160-171. 10.1093/sleep/10.2.160, 1987

Effect of Aging on Sleep-Related Changes in Respiratory Variables
  Karen H. Naifeh, John W. Severinghaus, Joe Kamiya
  Sleep, Volume 10, Issue 2, 1 March 1987, Pages 160–171

Summary of Payload Integration Plan (PIP) for Starlab-1 flight experiment
  Cowings, Patricia & Toscano, W & Kamiya, J & Miller, N & Sharp, J.
  National Aeronautics and Space Administration, Ames Research Center, Moffett
  Field, California, 1988

Effect of aging on estimates of hypercapnic ventilatory response during sleep
 H Naifeh, K & W Severinghaus, J & Kamiya, J & Krafft, M.
 Journal of Applied Physiology 66(4):1956-64 · May 1989

Final Report. Spacelab-3 Flight Experiment #3AFT23: Autogenic-Feedback Training As A Preventive Method for Space Adaptation Syndrome
 Cowings, Patricia & Toscano, Bill & Kamiya, Joe & E. Miller, Neal & C. Sharp, Joseph.
 National Aeronautics and Space Administration, Ames Research Center, Moffett Field, California, 1988

Altered autonomic function in patients with arthritis or with chronic myofascial pain
 Perry, Franklin & H. Heller, Philip & Kamiya, Joe & D. Levine, Jon
 Pain, 39(1), October 1989, pp 77–84

Biofeedback Methods and the Status of Subjective Experience in Human Biology
 Joe Kamiya
 Japanese Biofeedback Society, Nara Women's University, 1998

The First Communications About Operant Conditioning of the EEG
 Joe Kamiya
 Journal of Neurotherapy 15(1):65-73 · February 2011

Alpha-Theta Neurofeedback in the 21st Century: A Handbook for Clinicians and Researchers
 Antonio Martins-Mourao, Cynthia Kerson
 Foreword by: Joe Kamiya
 BMED Press, 2017

Joe Kamiya: Thinking Inside the Box

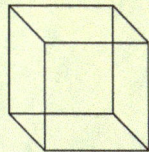

Thinking Inside the Box is an exquisite living interview of Joe Kamiya's life as a humanitarian, scientist and visionary. The authors brilliantly capture Joe's heart, mind and soul as they weave introspective discussion, historical and cultural content, imagination, and compassionate inquiry to remind us of the importance of honoring a personal science linked with objective exploration.

This will be a classic in the archives of understanding the evolution of biofeedback and neurofeedback.

Sal Barba, PhD, BCN
Co-founder of Island Center for Complementary Medicine
Seattle, Washington

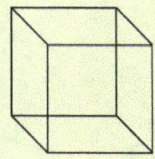

I met Joe in 1972 at the Biofeedback Research Society meeting in Monterey... and have gotten to know him slowly through the years. I have always known Joe to be a gentle thoughtful scientist, providing deep thoughtful replies to inquiries, giving time to everyone openly. Joe was so busy giving that it was only rarely and with the briefest of glimpses that I learned of his earlier days which led him to EEG and discrimination of the alpha state. He only rarely hinted at his time in internment, which may have helped lead to his deep introspection and interest in internal states. It was never about Joe... he thought deeply and not about personal fame/fortune. He asked the best questions. I recommend that all involved in biofeedback get this book and enjoy delving into the one of the true foundations of the field... the depth and passion of a pioneer... my dear friend, Joe Kamiya... as gently guided by the authors to share these riches with us all.

You will be a better person for reading it.

Jay Gunkelman, QEEGD Emeritus
Suisun City, CA

$34.99
ISBN 978-1-7349618-0-5

www.ingramcontent.com/pod-product-compliance
Lightning Source LLC
Chambersburg PA
CBHW070403240426
43661CB00056B/2516